# NOW THAT I HAVE BEEN BORN AGAIN, *What's Next?*

## BY KENNETH POLK

*Now That I Have Been Born Again, What's Next?*

Trilogy Christian Publishers A Wholly Owned Subsidiary of Trinity Broadcasting Network | 2442 Michelle Drive Tustin, CA 92780

Copyright © 2024 by Kenneth Polk

Unless otherwise indicated, Scripture quotations are taken from the King James Version of the Bible. Public domain. Scripture quotations marked AMP are taken from the Amplified® Bible (AMP), Copyright © 2015 by The Lockman Foundation. Used by permission. www.lockman.org. Scripture quotations marked NIV are taken from the Holy Bible, New International Version®, NIV®. Copyright © 1973, 1978, 1984, 2011 by Biblica, Inc.™ Used by permission of Zondervan. All rights reserved worldwide. www.zondervan.com. The "NIV" and "New International Version" are trademarks registered in the United States Patent and Trademark Office by Biblica, Inc.™ Scripture quotations marked NKJV are taken from the New King James Version®. Copyright © 1982 by Thomas Nelson. Used by permission. All rights reserved.

No part of this book may be reproduced, stored in a retrieval system, or transmitted by any means without written permission from the author. All rights reserved. Printed in the USA.

Rights Department, 2442 Michelle Drive, Tustin, CA 92780.

Trilogy Christian Publishing/TBN and colophon are trademarks of Trinity Broadcasting Network.

For information about special discounts for bulk purchases, please contact Trilogy Christian Publishing.

Trilogy Disclaimer: The views and content expressed in this book are those of the author and may not necessarily reflect the views and doctrine of Trilogy Christian Publishing or the Trinity Broadcasting Network.

10 9 8 7 6 5 4 3 2 1

Library of Congress Cataloging-in-Publication Data is available.

ISBN: 979-8-89333-273-5 | E-ISBN: 979-8-89333-274-2

# DEDICATION

This book is dedicated to all my brothers and sisters in Christ who have struggled in an area of their lives at one time or another. Many of you started this journey alone, having no idea of the life you were to live and no true Christian friends to guide you. However, you persevered and overcame your weakness, and you are now living a victorious life in Christ. Today you stand having this testimony: "For Christ's sake, I delight in weaknesses, in insults, in hardships, in persecutions, in difficulties. For when I am weak, then I am strong" (2 Corinthians 12:10 NIV).

# CONTENTS

Prologue . . . . . . . . . . . . . . . . . . . . . . . . . . . . . . . . 7

**Part 1**
**Understanding the Need for Salvation** . . . . . . . . . . 23

1. A Changed Life . . . . . . . . . . . . . . . . . . . . . . . . . 25
2. God Provides a Cure . . . . . . . . . . . . . . . . . . . . 37

**Part 2**
**A New Life Experience in Christ** . . . . . . . . . . . . . . . 57

3. The Beginning of a New Life Journey. . . . . . . . . . 59
4. The Work of the Holy Spirit in the
   Believer's Life. . . . . . . . . . . . . . . . . . . . . . . . . 67
5. Empowered to Live . . . . . . . . . . . . . . . . . . . . . . 79

**Part 3**
**Growing in Grace and the Knowledge of God** . . . . 89

6. Newborn Babies in Christ . . . . . . . . . . . . . . . . . 91
7. Child Training . . . . . . . . . . . . . . . . . . . . . . . . . 101
8. A Life in Transition . . . . . . . . . . . . . . . . . . . . . 111
9. Mortifying the Deeds of the Body . . . . . . . . . . . 119
10. The Renewing of the Mind . . . . . . . . . . . . . . . . 133
11. Growth through Knowledge . . . . . . . . . . . . . . . 145

**Part 4**
**Maintaining Your Relationship with God**. . . . . . . . 173

12. Living by Faith. . . . . . . . . . . . . . . . . . . . . . . . . 177
13. A Life of Persecution . . . . . . . . . . . . . . . . . . . . 189
14. Working Out Your Own Salvation . . . . . . . . . . . 199

# PROLOGUE

It is Sunday afternoon, and the pastor has just completed his sermon. The Word of God was rich today, and the presence of the Holy Spirit was moving throughout the worship service. When the altar call was given for individuals to come up who had never before been saved, immediately you approached the altar. The pastor ministered salvation to you, and you confessed and repented of your sins to God, asking Him to come into your heart. Instantly, Jesus Christ became your Lord and Savior. The benediction has now been given, and the worship service has concluded. You are still excited and filled with joy after accepting Jesus Christ as your Savior. People are walking up to you, welcoming you to the family. Some pause to share a few words of encouragement. Finally, you get into your car and drive home. You continue to think about your encounter with God and how good you feel. You know your life has changed. Something miraculous and supernatural has taken place within you, although you cannot totally explain it.

The next morning you awaken and begin your day, when suddenly it hits you, and you ask yourself, *Now that I have been born again, what's next?*

## Now That I Have Been Born Again, *What's Next?*

This is the question so many new believers in Christ are confronted with. Over the years of being saved, ministering to others, and currently holding a pastoral office, I have had the opportunity to observe many new Christian converts struggle with transitioning their lives. Yes, the Bible tells us, "If any man be in Christ, he is a new creature: old things are passed away; behold, all things are become new" (2 Corinthians 5:17). And yet so many find themselves asking the question Nicodemus asked, when he said to Jesus, "How can these things be?" (John 3:9).

While you know you are now a new creation in Christ, the dilemma you are confronted with is laying aside the old life, with all its sinful habits, and learning to live a new life in Christ. Moreover, you have no idea what this new life entails. A new Christian convert is at a vulnerable stage of their spiritual life because they are babies in Christ. Personally, I feel the first six months to a year after receiving Christ as your Savior will begin to clearly define your Christian walk. This time frame is crucial because during this period, the new convert will either begin a growth cycle, or they will backslide and return to the old life from which they were delivered. Simply put, they will either live or die spiritually. We will explore this more deeply in Part 3 of this book, entitled "Growing Up Spiritually."

## Prologue

The key to true spiritual development is the foundation upon which you are building, and who is sowing into your life. Furthermore, the spiritual environment in which you are raised up will have a great influence on your new life in Christ. From the day we were born, the sin nature, which dwells within the flesh, taught us all the wrong things. All of humanity has inherited this sinful nature through Adam's act of disobedience. In Genesis, the Bible describes fallen man's intellectual framework this way: "And God saw that the wickedness of man was great in the earth, and that every imagination of the thoughts of his heart was only evil continually" (Genesis 6:5). So, through the Great Flood, God killed all life that was upon the earth—except for Noah and his family and the animals that were safe within the ark.

After the waters of the flood had subsided, God reaffirmed this behavior pattern within the minds of men. After Noah departed the ark, God said, "I will not again curse the ground any more for man's sake; for the imagination of man's heart is evil from his youth" (Genesis 8:21). Each human being, because of the sin nature, is born with a mind that is corrupt and in a state of rebellion toward God. The word "mind" comes from the Greek word *nous*, meaning "the organ of mental perception, apprehension, or intellectual framework." Before you were saved, your intellectual framework was flawed and not receptive to the Word of God.

That takes us back to the question: How do I lay down the old life, so I can effectively live this new life in Christ? A better way of asking this is: How can I unlearn all that I have learned about the old life, which was sinful, and then learn to live a life of holiness? The answer is that a renewing, or renovating, of the mind must take place. The old mindset must be demolished, and the walls of your mind must be rebuilt with the Word of God as its foundation. We will discuss this more in depth in chapter 10 of this book.

I want to pause a moment to define two words according to the *Webster's New College Dictionary*. These two words will be referred to often in this work. The first is *transition*. *Transition* is defined as "a passing from one condition, form, or one stage to another; the period of such passing." Once a man or woman receives Christ as his or her personal Savior, according to Scripture, they are "delivered . . . from the power of darkness, and [is] translated . . . into the kingdom of his dear Son" (Colossians 1:13); thus, we see the need to conform to a new life that is Christ-centered.

The second word is *discipline*. *Discipline* is defined as "training expected to produce a specific character or pattern of behavior, especially training that produces moral

## Prologue

or mental improvement." The Lord Jesus said, "If ye continue in my word, then are ye my disciples indeed; and ye shall know the truth, and the truth shall make you free" (John 8:31–32). A true disciple of Christ is a disciplined person. He or she has become disciplined in the things of God. We will discuss this more under the heading "Child Training" in chapter 7 of this book.

The purpose I had in writing this book is to help new converts avoid some of the pitfalls I experienced after I was saved. Understand this: the enemy of your soul, the devil, is not pleased with the decision you made in forsaking him and turning to God. So, consequently, he is going to do everything in his power to destroy you, or kill you, spiritually. The devil can only achieve this by using fleshly desires to lure you into committing acts of sin. Sin will always cause a breach in your relationship with God.

The devil will use family, friends, your job, and sadly some of the people sitting right next to you every Sunday morning in church. Yes, the devil goes to church! Just because a person belongs to a church, or is a member of a church, that does not mean they have been born again or are saved. We must constantly be aware of predators of the soul, those who will attempt to hinder our spiritual growth and drain the spiritual life from us.

## Now That I Have Been Born Again, *What's Next?*

### The Power of a Witness

In my late teenage years and early twenties, I dated a young lady named Sharon. After about a year after we began dating, Sharon gave her life to Jesus Christ. She would always invite me to church and impress upon me the need to be saved. Every opportunity she had, the Lord would use her to speak a word into my spirit. The more she shared the love of God with me, the more it became apparent I needed Him, and it became more difficult for me to resist Him. So finally, one Sunday, I went to Sharon's church. The late Bishop Anderson preached a powerful message from the Word of God, and at the conclusion of his sermon, the bishop gave an altar call for those who desired to be saved. I was not ready to give my life to Christ at that moment, but God still had a message for me—and He began to speak through Bishop Anderson. Standing at the foot of the altar, Bishop said, "There is someone here who's not ready to surrender to Christ, but if you would come and shake my hand, it will be alright." I said within myself, *I can do that.* So, I stood up and began to walk toward the altar. But as I did so, suddenly, I experienced my first "God encounter" in the form of a vision. As I started down the aisle, the floor on which I was walking on became as clouds, and it seemed as if everything was happening in slow motion.

## Prologue

There, before me, was a golden gate, which swung open from the center, with two angelic beings standing at each side of this open gate. These angels begin to beckon to me with their hands to come in. As I reached the altar and shook Bishop Anderson's hand, the vision ceased. After leaving church that day, I experienced a sense of peace and love within my spirit that I had never felt before. Being a troubled young man, I had tried everything I could find to fill the emptiness within my life. God was showing me He could give me the love and peace I had been longing for if I gave my life to Him; however, I was still not ready.

A month later, I was in the barbershop getting my hair done. Samantha, the hairstylist, set me under the hair dryer. While I sat there, I looked around for something to read. I picked up this book titled *The Fool* and began to read to pass the time. In it, it told the story of a king who owned all the riches in the land. This king had a jester who would always make him laugh. One day the king summoned the jester to the palace and said to him, "You are the biggest fool I know. I am going to give you this golden staff, and I want you to search the countryside to see if you can find a bigger fool than yourself. If you do, I want you to give him the golden staff." So, the jester departed the palace in search of a bigger fool than himself. Meanwhile, while he was away, the king became sick unto death, and he sent word for the jester to return. Upon his arrival, the jester asked the king what was wrong, and the king responded, "I am going on a journey from which I'm never going to return." The jester asked, "Are you prepared for your journey?" The king responded that he was not. The jester returned the golden staff to him and said, "You are the biggest fool I know."

The next page closed the book with these two questions: "Are you prepared for your journey?" and "Have you made Jesus Christ your Lord and Savior?" I closed the book and drifted off to sleep, but in my subconscious mind, what I read troubled me. I awoke to an anxiety attack, and then I fell out in the barber shop. They rushed me to the hospital, where I called my mother. When she arrived, the first words she uttered were, "The Lord is just whipping you." I really did not need to hear that from her at that moment. After I had sat there a while, my vital signs stabilized, and I signed myself out of the hospital and went home.

I was saved in June 1978 at Anderson Memorial Church of God in Christ, where Sharon worshiped. I was twenty-one years old when the Lord saved me. I will never forget that day nor the circumstances surrounding it. After signing myself out of the hospital that Saturday, I just took it easy and laid around the house the reminder of the day.

## Prologue

On Sunday morning, I woke up around 9 a.m., and as I lay there in the bed, in my spirit I could hear the Lord speaking to me, saying, *Get up and go to church.* However, there was another voice, the devil, which kept saying, *You do not need to go to church.* This battle continued for several hours. Suddenly, I jumped up and said to myself, "I'm going to church!" I got dressed and began pondering, *Where should I go?* Then I heard a voice say, *Go back to Sharon's church.*

It was a very overcast day, and thunderstorms were in the forecast. I arrived at Anderson Memorial around 12:20, and Bishop Anderson was in the middle of preaching his Sunday sermon. The lights in the church were on, but the natural lighting outside made it look somewhat dark inside. As I sat there, the devil told me to get up and leave. I got up, walked out of the sanctuary, and went downstairs. But then I stood there a moment and said, "No, I'm going to stay here and deal with this." So, I turned around, went back into the sanctuary, and sat down. At the conclusion of the message, Bishop Anderson gave an altar call for those who desired to be saved. At first, I sat there, but then suddenly it felt as if my heart was being pulled from my chest and drawn toward the altar. I felt that if I had continued to sit there, I would have had a heart attack. So, I left my seat and approached the altar.

## Now That I Have Been Born Again, *What's Next?*

When I reached the altar, one of the elders approached me and began to speak with me about Jesus and how He saves us from sin. He explained how much Jesus loves me and how He shed His blood, died, and rose from the dead three days later. He continued by expounding on the importance of confessing and repenting of my sins, how my sins could be washed away by the blood of Jesus. Then the elder began to pray with me. With my hands lifted and my eyes closed, I begin to confess and repent of my sins, calling on the name of Jesus. Suddenly, I could see a bright light all around me, shining in me and through me. The devil tried to distract me by saying, *The sun is out—now you can have some fun when you leave here.* At that moment, I opened my eyes, but the church was just as gloomy-looking as it had been prior to me going to the altar. So I closed my eyes and continued to pray. The bright light I had experienced was still present.

Afterward, I shared my testimony and returned to my seat. After the benediction, I started toward the front door to leave. I placed my hand on the door to push it open, but then suddenly I heard the voice of the Lord. His voice was so powerful it immediately caught my attention. I stood still. He said to me, *This is a new beginning—go out and face the world.* My life has never been the same since that day. I thank God for Sharon's obedience, as He constantly

## Prologue

compelled her to share the Gospel massage with me. I never made Anderson Memorial my church home, although I should have. I decided to follow my mother and sister and become a member of their church. The first lesson I quickly learned as a new Christian convert was to grow where God has planted you, and not where you plant yourself.

As a young Christian or baby in Christ, I was not raised in the best spiritual environment. I am not alluding to my home, but I am referring to the church I was attending. My mother's church, which I am not going to name, had a choir that was filled with young people. However, the conduct of many of them was worse than some of the people I knew from the streets. Many of them were carnal. They would party, drink, use profanity, commit fornication, and even fight. Their mental framework had not changed. There was no spiritual fruit.

I never understood how single young ladies who sang in the choir or held other positions within the church could become pregnant by guys in the church and nothing was said or done to address the sin issues. The young ladies would sing throughout their pregnancies, have their babies, and then return to the choir. The young men who impregnated them never faced any discipline. Also, some young men and women were living a homosexual lifestyle while still functioning in church leadership positions. As time passed, I discovered the atmosphere there was not conducive for true spiritual growth. Thus, I often felt like a deer in the headlights, not knowing which way to go or to whom to turn.

The second lesson I quickly learned was to be careful of whom I allowed to speak over my life or to sow within my spirit. Just because a person is ministering does not mean they have been divinely appointed by God to do so. There is a distinct difference between a true pastor, who has been called and appointed by God, and a hireling. According to Jesus, a hireling really is not concerned about the well-being of the sheep (John 10:12–13). (I will speak more from these passages of Scripture in chapter 6.) A hireling is more concerned with how he can fleece the sheep, using the people for his own financial gain. In this season, people are going online and obtaining ministerial credentials without ever being called or appointed by God. Many teach in the church without any true spiritual revelation of the Scriptures. Therefore, it is imperative that we are able to distinguish a true pastor from a hireling. For a hireling, ministry is just a job; however, for the one who has been called by God, it is a way of life, a labor of love. A true pastor "under shepherd" is concerned about your spiritual well-being and will not compromise the truth of

## Prologue

the Gospel, nor ignore sin.

When a person is teaching or preaching, they are sowing seeds into your soul and your spirit. The question now becomes: What type of seeds are being sown? Jesus, while explaining to His disciples the parable of the sower, stated, "The sower soweth the word" (Mark 4:14). A true sower will teach or preach a pure, unadulterated message. They will not add, take away, or compromise the truth of God's Word. Neither will they use the Word of God deceitfully, to support their own agenda. They understand the necessity of teaching the truth. The truth of the Scriptures will bring us to spiritual liberty and maturity. Keep in mind the importance of Scripture as we begin this new journey. Paul wrote: "All scripture is given by inspiration of God, and is profitable for doctrine, for reproof, for correction, for instruction in righteousness: That the man of God may be perfect, thoroughly furnished unto all good works" (2 Timothy 3:16–17). God is all about creating disciples and transforming lives!

The preached Word is not meant for entertainment. God's Word is preached to help you develop true Christian character and help you understand and learn what God requires of you as a Christian. As I stated earlier, your spiritual environment, the "church where you worship," will have a huge influence on your spiritual life. If it is healthy, you will have a greater opportunity to develop into a true disciple. If it is not healthy, however, there may be areas of your life in which you struggle. The bottom line is, at the end of the day, you will become a product of the spiritual environment in which you are raised in.

For several years after becoming saved, I struggled with fornication. I am being very transparent, because many Christians—even those in leadership positions—act as if they have never struggled with sin in any area of their Christian life. I struggled because no one told me that it was wrong, nor was any emphasis from the pulpit placed on living a life of holiness. Eventually, through reading and studying the Scriptures, the Lord revealed to me that was not the way God intended for me to live. I was saved, truly in love with the Lord, yet I was still in bondage in this area of my life. Having knowledge of the truth brought me under conviction and spiritual scrutiny. It also intensified the struggle between my flesh and my spirit. My flesh wanted me to serve it; however, my spirit wanted to be obedient to God and His Word. The enemy of my soul had erected a spiritual stronghold that had to be uprooted and destroyed. Daily, I thank God for liberating me—and for His patience as I become victorious in that area of my life.

## Prologue

Due to my personal experience and love for God's people, I am driven and committed to equipping new converts with the truth of God's Word. As a new Christian, it is absolutely necessary that you build a strong foundation from the beginning. It is equally important that you become disciplined in your thought process and your walk in Christ, submitting to the Holy Spirit and becoming obedient to God's Word. Remember, character building and spiritual growth are part of a process that does not happen overnight. Find a strong, Bible-teaching church and a mentor or life coach with whom you feel comfortable talking, someone who will help you maximize your life in Christ. The goal is not to be the best you can be; the aim is to become all that *God* saved you for and created you to be. I pray this book will help you answer the question, Now that I have been born again, what's next?

# PART ONE

*Understanding the Need for Salvation*

# CHAPTER 1

## *A Changed Life*

As you embark on this wonderful Christian life, it is imperative that you understand your new life is all about change. You cannot continue to live a sinful life and expect to have a healthy relationship with God. The *Webster's New College Dictionary* states, "Change denotes a making or becoming distinctly different and implies either a radical transmutation of character or replacement with something else: It also added, to cause to become different; alter; transform; convert." The Scriptures tell us, "Therefore if any man be in Christ, he is a new creature: old things are passed away; behold, all things are become new" (2 Corinthians 5:17). It is much like the caterpillar, which, at its appointed time, finds a branch and spins a silk "sleeping bag" from the silk gland of its mouth, called a cocoon. Once the cocoon is completed, within it and beyond the unseeing eye, the caterpillar makes a complete metamorphosis and later emerges as a beautiful butterfly.

The believing, repenting sinner, now immersed in Christ and beyond the unseeing eye, is being changed, or converted, within their inner man from a sinner to a saint, from death to life. The believer has become a new creation in Christ. The apostle Paul stated that we are "created in Christ Jesus" (Ephesians 2:10). The word "created" here is from the Greek word *kitzo*, which is equivalent to the Hebrew word *bara*, used for "created" in Genesis 1:27. God is the subject of both words, because only God can create. God is all about transforming your life. The born-again believer in Christ is changed from a life that was sinful and self-motivated, void of the presence of God, to a life that is empowered and influenced by the Holy Spirit and God's Word.

All humanity is born knowing only the sin nature, and it shapes our personality, character, and motivations. Under the influence of this sinful nature, we are separated from God and the God-kind of life. Consequently, in this condition, mankind had no relationship with God. Therefore, man had to be saved and his sins forgiven in order to be reconciled to God. Let us examine the character of the un-regenerated man who is under the influence of the sin nature.

## The Old Man

To help understand the radical change you have experienced, you must first understand the life from which you have been delivered. The apostle Paul, in his letter to the

## A Changed Life

church at Ephesus, gives us a clear understanding of that life: "And you hath he quickened, who were dead in trespasses and sins; wherein in times past ye walked according to the course of this world, according to the prince of the power of the air, the spirit that now worketh in the children of disobedience: Among whom also we all had our conversation in times past in the lusts of our flesh, fulfilling the desires of the flesh and of the mind; and were by nature the children of wrath, even as others" (Ephesians 2:1–3).

The writer, Paul, in the first verse uses the word *quicken*. This word means "to make alive." This *quickening* is the work of the Holy Spirit, as He imparts spiritual life to the believing, repenting sinner. I will address this work in greater detail in chapter 4. Prior to this quickening, the unbeliever is described as dead. This is not referring to physical death, but spiritual death—simply, separation from God and the God kind of life. What caused this spiritual death? Trespasses and sins. Trespasses, meaning to depart from truth or to not be willing to obey the truth of God's Word. "Sin" is from the Greek word *hamartia*, defined as a "missing of the mark," thus falling short of God's Word. The unbeliever lives a life that is not in alignment with God's truth, thus falling short of the standard that God has established for humanity.

In the second and third verses, the writer, Paul, describes the spiritual condition resulting from being dead in trespasses and sins. Note that in both verses he uses the words "in time past," referring to a life prior to being saved. The word *walked* here refers to lifestyle or the way one lives, their behavior or conduct. The unsaved person's life is regulated by trespasses and sin. Paul continues to describe this fallen condition in the second and third verses, which I will paraphrase. Prior to coming to Christ, we lived in accordance with this world system, under the influence of the forces of darkness. These evil powers govern the children of disobedience, and their ordered behavior was in the lust of the flesh. Driven by sinful passions, they sought to fulfill the cravings of the flesh and their evil desires and were children of wrath by nature. Thus, the un-regenerated individual is a child of disobedience by choice and a child of wrath by nature, because they are born sinners.

## How Did Humanity Get to This Point?

Contrary to the belief of many, God did not create mankind to be sinners as we are today. Adam was created "a living soul" (Genesis 2:7). However, Adam's disobedience to God's revealed will brought about a ruinous change in his total being and generated within him the sin force. This

## A Changed Life

cataclysmic result also extended to all mankind. Scripture tells us, "By one man sin entered into the world, and death by sin, and so death passed upon all men, for that all have sinned" (Romans 5:12). God created Adam after His image and likeness (see Genesis 1:26–27). (We will further examine this under the heading "Identity Crisis.") Adam was created as a spiritual being, having eternal life. Therefore, he could eat of the Tree of Life at that time. After his fall, God dispatched cherubim and a flaming sword that turned in every direction to prevent him from eating of it and living forever in his sin (see Genesis 3:24).

Adam willingly chose to violate God's revealed will. God had explicitly commanded him not to eat of the Tree of the Knowledge of Good and Evil; if he ate of it, he would surely die (see Genesis 2:17). Furthermore, the result of Adam's single act of sin thrust him and all mankind into spiritual death. Remember, spiritual and physical death were not part of God's creation, nor were they part of His plan for man. Neither was hatred, envy, jealousy, murder, and the like. These are the effects of sin. Adam was created knowing only life—spiritual life, the God kind of life—but he forfeited it all the moment he sinned. As believers, we must understand the strain that sin places on our relationship with God and abstain from it. Simply put, sin separates us from God, and separation from God is spiritual death. Let examine how Adam's sin affected all humanity and caused man to lose his true identity.

## Identity Crisis

*Identity* is defined by the *Webster's New College Dictionary* as the "condition or fact of being the same or exactly alike; sameness in characteristics and qualities." The book of Genesis states, "God said, Let us make man in our image, after our likeness: and let them have dominion over the fish of the sea, and over the fowl of the air, and over the cattle, and over all the earth, and over every creeping thing that creepeth upon the earth" (Genesis 1:26).

I would like to take a moment to focus on the words *image* and *likeness*. These two words define the identity and the character of the man God was creating. The word *image* is a translation of the Hebrew word *selem*, meaning "the shadow outline of a figure." This word is not speaking of a physical image, but a spiritual one. So, we see that the relationship between God and Adam was spiritual. God is spirit, and being created in the image of God, Adam was created as a spirit likewise. Jesus once said, "God is a Spirit: and they that worship him must worship him in spirit and in truth" (John 4:24).

## A Changed Life

God took a lump of clay from the earth and made a figurine of a body. The body lay lifeless until the breath, or the Spirit of Life, was breathed into it. At that point, the body became animated, and man became a living soul. The Bible confirms this, as the Scripture states, "And the LORD God formed man of the dust of the ground, and breathed into his nostrils the breath of life; and man became a living soul" (Genesis 2:7). Note, Adam is characterized as being a "living soul," created in the likeness and image of God, and not a human being. Adam's sin caused separation from God. No longer a living soul, he was now influenced by the sinful nature that was residing in his flesh. He was now considered a "human being," or a "creature of the flesh." The essence of man is not the body; it is the spirit, or the inner man. The body gives us an outward display of the inward machinery of the soul and spirit. Simply put, what we see a person do, what they say, and how they respond is the direct result of the activity within the soul and spirit.

The word *likeness* is the translation of the Hebrew word *damuth*, meaning the "correspondence or resemblance of that shadow to the figure." Adam was created having many of God's attributes; he was morally and spiritually pure. Simply put, Adam was holy, righteous, and sinless. He even had eternal life. There was no sin, evil, or anything that was impure in his character. This cannot be stressed enough. We live in an age when people do not want to deal with the fact that Christians must be holy, morally pure, and daily seek to live a sinless life.

Throughout Scripture, God is pictured as being holy. For example, the Word tells us about the angels: "And one cried unto another, and said, Holy, holy, holy, is the LORD of hosts" (Isaiah 6:3). Likewise, God requires every believer to be holy. While exhorting the saints concerning living a holy life, Peter quoted Leviticus 19:2, when he said, "Because it is written, Be ye holy; for I am holy" (1 Peter 1:16). I know today some people have a problem with the idea of living holy lives and practicing spiritual purity, but committing acts of sin is a choice, and the soul that sins shall surely die. I will address this further in chapter 8.

The first man, Adam, in soul and spirit was in perfect synchronization with God. Adam being morally and spiritually pure, worshiped God, and had a close relationship with Him. Adam was also highly intelligent, as he named every animal species (Genesis 2:19–20). We could say he had the "mind of God." Paul wrote, "Let this mind be in you, which was also in Christ Jesus" (Philippians 2:5). However, he now found himself in an identity crisis because he had forfeited his identity because of disobedi-

## A Changed Life

ence. Furthermore, Paul told the church at Corinth, "But we have the mind of Christ" (1 Corinthians 2:16). Adam thought as God thought—and just as every born-again believer should think, which is as Christ thinks.

Several years ago, someone became financially secure when they came up with the acronym *WWJD*, meaning, *What Would Jesus Do?* To respond to life's temptations in the manner Jesus did, you would have to think as He thought.

Being omniscient, God knew Adam would transgress His revealed will and lose his identity, but that was not God's plan for his life. Neither was it God's plan for all humanity to be born sinful and separated from Him and from the God kind of life. Being the federal head of humanity, Adam's sinful act thrust all humanity into a life of sin and death. Again, sin was not part of God's creation or plan for man. No longer influenced by God, men wander aimlessly throughout life's journey enslaved to sin and death because of Adam's transgression. There were no laws in place to govern God's relationship with men. Scripture tells us this in Romans:

> For until the law sin was in the world: but sin is not imputed when there is no law. Nevertheless, death reigned from Adam to Moses, even over them that had not sinned

after the similitude of Adams transgression, who is the figure of him that was to come.

**—Romans 5:13–14**

God had told Adam not to eat of the Tree of the Knowledge of Good and Evil. That was His revealed will. This one command governed God's relationship with Adam. When Adam transgressed God's revealed will, he lost his identity and forfeited all that God had created for him. Sin permeated humanity, but sin could not be imputed, meaning "added to one's personal account" because there were no laws in place to govern God's relationship with mankind. Nevertheless, spiritual death, which was caused by sin, reigned in the earth from Adam to Moses, even over those who had not sinned after the likeness of Adam's transgression.

On Mount Sinai, God gave Moses the Law, the Ten Commandments (Exodus 20:1–17). These laws were established to govern His relationship with the children of Israel, which the people agreed to keep. When a person violated the law, that sin was added to the individual person's account. However, the law did not provide a cure for sin. Men were still spiritually dead, corrupt, and separated from God. The difference now is that men were aware

## A Changed Life

of their sins as they had willfully violated God's revealed will.

However, God had a plan that would put an end to the reign of sin and bring forth reconciliation to those who trusted in Jesus through faith and by faith. Jesus would provide this cure by His sacrificial death on the cross.

# CHAPTER 2

## *God Provides a Cure for Sin*

As a new believer In Christ Jesus, it is essential that you begin to build on a solid foundation. Therefore, I am taking time in the first two chapters of this book to give a synopsis of Adam's act of disobedience, which affected everyone. Even though Adam sinned, God had a plan for salvation and reconciliation for mankind through His Son, Jesus. So often people find it difficult to transition from their old, sinful habits to a life of spiritual liberty in Christ. Knowledge is powerful, and what you do not know can literally kill you spiritually. God will never justify acts of sin nor condone sin. Your eternal resting place is at stake, so let's continue.

> For the life of the flesh is in the blood:
> and I have given it to you upon the altar
> to make atonement for your souls: for it is
> the blood that maketh an atonement for the
> soul.
>
> —**Leviticus 17:11**

While Moses was on Mount Sinai obtaining the Ten Commandments, also known as the Law, God gave him instructions, or a blueprint, to construct a tabernacle (see Exodus 25). God instructed the people to make a sanctuary where He could dwell among them or in the midst of them. This tabernacle had to be built according to the pattern He had given. Man was not allowed to deviate from the pattern (Exodus 25:8–9).

According to Exodus 26:31–37, the tabernacle was divided by two veils, or curtains. One was placed before the door of the holy place, or the sanctuary, and the second curtain separated the sanctuary, or holy place, from the Holy of Holies. Upon completion of the tabernacle, on a day designated by God called the Day of Atonement, the high priest would go behind the curtain into the Holy of Holies with the blood of animals to make atonement for himself and the sins of the people. The writer of the book of Hebrews, in the ninth and tenth chapters, gives us a detailed account of the tabernacle services, its yearly bloody sacrifices, and Jesus Christ's fulfillment of the high priestly duties. Let's examine several passages of Scripture from the ninth chapter of Hebrews.

> Then verily the first covenant had also ordinances of divine service, and a worldly sanctuary, for there was a tabernacle made; the first, wherein was the candlestick, and the table, of shewbread; which is called

the sanctuary. And after the second veil, the tabernacle which is called the Holiest of all; which had the golden censer, and the ark of the covenant overlaid round about with gold, wherein was the golden pot that had manna, and Aaron's rod that budded, and the tables of the covenant; and over it the cherubims of glory shadowing the mercyseat.

**—Hebrews 9:1–5**

As stated, the tabernacle was divided into two parts. When you entered through the first veil or curtain, you entered the sanctuary, also known as the holy place. The priest, as well as the people, could enter the sanctuary. In this sanctuary, or holy place, according to Hebrews 6:10, the priest performed a religious service. The writer called it a "worldly sanctuary," implying that it was made by men.

I want to take a moment to address this phrase "worldly sanctuary," or church building. From 2020 to late 2022, the world was under siege by COVID-19. This global pandemic touched all humanity, no matter where you lived on earth. It was as if God put everyone on punishment or in time-out and told us all to go to our rooms because of our disobedience. God in His own time will eventually judge humanity because of our sin, our constant rebellion, and our transgression of His will.

## Now That I Have Been Born Again, *What's Next?*

During the pandemic, nearly all commerce came to an abrupt stop. Parishioners were not permitted to enter their local churches or sanctuaries due to the stay-at-home mandates imposed by the government. Over time, many begin to say that they could not wait for the churches to reopen, as if their relationship with God hinged on them returning to a building. They did not understand that every born-again believer in Christ Jesus is the Church. The church building is simply a place where we gather to fellowship with one another. It is a worldly sanctuary. The building itself is nothing, no matter how elaborate or state of the art it may be; it is just a building. Sadly, in some cases it is used as a place to gather for worship in the morning, and a bingo hall in the evening. In the book of Acts, Stephen and Paul addressed the temple that those people of that day admired:

> But Solomon built him an house. Howbeit the most High dwelleth not in temples made with hands.
>
> —**Acts 7:47–48**

> God that made the world and all things therein, seeing that he is Lord of heaven and earth, dwelleth not in temples made with hands.
>
> —**Acts 17:24**

## God Provides a Cure for Sin

In these two passages of Scripture, Stephen and Paul emphasized that God does not dwell in man-made temples, synagogues, or church buildings. Scripture makes it known to us that "ye are the temple of God, and that the Spirit of God dwelleth in you? If any man defile the temple of God, him shall God destroy; for the temple of God is holy, which temple ye are" (1 Corinthians 3:16–17). The true Church is the body of Christ; it is His temple, His dwelling place. The word "church," *ekklesia*, means "called-out ones," those who have been saved, blood-washed, and Spirit-filled. The Church is not a building, but a living organism, a spiritual body of believers. Unlike many today, the apostle Paul never thought of the Church as a physical structure, but as a dedicated group of disciples of Jesus Christ whom He purchased with His own blood and saved.

We have become too dependent on man, and his buildings, to guide us in spiritual matters instead of trusting the Holy Spirit and God's Word. When people congregate in the local church, if the Holy Spirit's presence is not abiding within them, it is just a building filled with people. There will be no power, anointing, healing, or deliverance. It is the people who bring God's presence with them. Due to the absence of the Holy Spirit and faith within many of the congregants, there is a power shortage within today's Church. Therefore, miracles are not taking place, people are not being healed, demons are not being cast out, and souls are not being saved. We have developed a routine or ritual of going to a building every Sunday, yet we are not experiencing God's power to produce a life-altering experience.

Having this complacency while going to a worldly "church building" and not understanding that we are the Church, many do not seek to enter beyond the second veil into the Holy of Holies—into God's presence. It is in His presence that change, healing, deliverance, and miracles are initiated and take place. The apostle Paul wrote, "Let us therefore come boldly unto the throne of grace, that we may obtain mercy, and find grace to help in time of need" (Hebrews 4:16).

As we continue to look at various passages in the ninth and tenth chapters of Hebrews, I want to paraphrase the details of the tabernacle services, the high priest duties, and its blood sacrifices. Under the Levitical system, during the yearly tabernacle service, only the high priest could enter through the second veil into the Holy of Holies, the holiest place of all. On the Day of Atonement, the high priest alone would enter the Holy of Holies with a sin offering. This was a long, arduous day for the high priest as he performed his high priestly duties. If he made a misstep or

## God Provides a Cure for Sin

did anything incorrectly, he would be struck down, simply killed by God. Therefore, a rope was tied around his waist to pull his body out in the event this happened. The robe he wore had bells on it. As he worked, the bells would jingle, which was an indication that he was still alive.

The blood used for the sin offering and for atonement came from either calves or goats that had been sacrificed (see Hebrews 9:12–13). (I will go more in depth on the high priestly duties under the heading "The High Priestly Ministry of Jesus.") While this annual work of the high priest was in force, the Holy Spirit indicated that the way into the holiest place of all—God's presence—was not yet revealed or opened while this earthly tabernacle was yet standing. Why? Sin stands between God and man, and the blood of bulls and goats could not purge the conscience from sin and dead works. The writer of Hebrews declared:

> For the law having a shadow of good things to come, and not the very image of the things, can never with those sacrifices which they offered year by year continually make the comers thereunto perfect. For then would they not have ceased to be offered? because that the worshippers once purged should have had no more conscience of sins. But in those sacrifices there is a remembrance again made of sins

every year. For it is not possible that the blood of bulls and of goats should take away sins.

—**Hebrews 10:1–4**

These yearly sacrifices and blood atonements could not rid man from the sin nature nor purge his conscience so there would be no more remembrance of sin. Thus, there was the need for yearly sacrifices that only covered their sins, but did not rid or deliver man from the sin nature. The Day of Atonement, with its blood sacrifices, was a shadow, or type, of better things to come, which would be fulfilled through Jesus Christ and His blood.

## The High Priestly Ministry of Jesus

Though Christ was a Priest, He did not perform priestly duties in the temple at Jerusalem. He taught there, but He never offered sacrifices or burned incense. His priesthood was not earthly, but heavenly, in the spiritual realm. As our spiritual High Priest, Jesus was able to achieve something no one else could—provide a cure for sin by means of His own blood, which reconciled us to God.

On the Day of Atonement, the high priestly duties were first to kill the sacrificial animal. This was an animal set

## God Provides a Cure for Sin

aside from birth for the purpose of being sacrificed. The blood drained from that animal would be taken by the high priest into the Holy of Holies and sprinkled upon the mercy seat seven times, thus making atonement for sin. Remember, "the life of the flesh is in the blood: and I have given it to you upon the altar to make an atonement for your souls: for it is the blood that maketh an atonement for the soul" (Leviticus 17:11).

In the twelfth chapter of Exodus, under the dispensation of promise, we see God implementing the Passover. You may be thinking, *Why is he discussing Passover?* The answer is, because Jesus was in Jerusalem to celebrate the Passover the week He was crucified. It was there on Calvary that Jesus, our High Priest, offered Himself as the Paschal Lamb for the sins of the people. The Passover, also known as the Feast of Unleavened Bread, was a High Sabbath day (see John 19:31). In the book of Exodus, God commanded the nation of Israel to keep the Passover yearly to commemorate their exodus from Egypt and His judgment upon that land.

> It is the LORD's passover. For I will pass through the land of Egypt this night, and will smite all the firstborn in the land of Egypt, both man and beast; and against all the gods of Egypt I will execute judgment:

I am the LORD. And the blood shall be to you for a token upon the houses where ye are: and when I see the blood, I will pass over you, and the plague shall not be upon you to destroy you, when I smite the land of Egypt. And this day shall be unto you for a memorial; and ye shall keep it a feast to the LORD throughout your generations; ye shall keep it a feast by an ordinance for ever.

—**Exodus 12:11–14**

Passover and the Day of Atonement (Yom Kippur) are inextricably bound together, or connected, in that both involve reconciliation through blood. As I previously stated, on the Day of Atonement, the high priest would sacrifice calves or goats, using their blood to make atonement for the sins of the people. However, the animal sacrificed for the Passover was a lamb, and it was the blood of the lamb that was to be placed upon the lintel and side posts of each house. The only thing that protected the children of Israel from the destroyer was the blood. When the spirit of death saw the blood, he passed over that house. The lamb was used as the Passover sacrifice, as the Word states, "Draw out and take you a lamb according to your families, and kill the passover" (Exodus 12:21). In 1 Corinthians 5:7, Christ is said to be our "passover," sacrificed for us.

## God Provides a Cure for Sin

This Passover lamb could not be just any lamb. It had to be without blemish. Simply put, it had to be without any kind of defect, unimpaired. It had to be a male within a year old (Exodus 12:5), roasted whole, with the head and all entrails and limbs attached. This lamb was a type of Christ. In describing Jesus, John the Baptist cried out, "Behold the Lamb of God, which taketh away the sin of the world" (John 1:29). While on the Isle of Patmos, receiving the Revelation of Jesus Christ, the apostle John described Jesus as a Lamb that had been slain (Revelation 5:6–8).

Jesus was holy, without any blemish. He was sinless, having no moral taint, thus He was the perfect sacrifice. As the Lamb of God, Jesus bore our sins in His body, which was sacrificed for all humanity. The apostle Peter referred to this fact as he wrote, "Who his own self bare our sins in his own body on the tree, that we, being dead to sins, should live unto righteousness: by whose stripes ye were healed" (1 Peter 2:24). The prophet Isaiah also wrote:

> Surely he hath borne our griefs, and carried our sorrows: yet we did esteem him stricken, smitten of God, and afflicted. But he was wounded for our transgressions, he was bruised for our iniquities: the chastisement of our peace was upon him; and with his stripes we are healed.
>
> **—Isaiah 53:4–5**

This selfless act of love by Jesus has given us victory over the sin nature. Due to Him being our substitute, bearing our sins in His body, the sin nature has been rendered powerless in the life of the believer in Christ. The apostle Paul wrote in Romans 6:6, "Knowing this, that our old man is crucified with him, that the body of sin might be destroyed, that henceforth we should not serve sin." Knowing this will be beneficial to you as you go through tests and temptations in this life; you will be able to walk in victory over the flesh.

As our High Priest, Jesus Himself entered the heavenly Holy of Holies and presented His own blood before God in the heavenly sanctuary. He did not enter the earthly tabernacle, as other high priests did on the Day of Atonement, but into heaven. The writer of Hebrews tells us:

> For Christ is not entered into the holy places made with hands, which are the figures of the true, but into heaven itself, now to appear in the presence of God for us.
>
> —Hebrews 9:24

When examining the salvation process and the works of God, we must keep in mind that these events are spiritual and have their origin in the spirit or heavenly realm. These events are not of this world system, nor earthly, or implemented by man. I want to place emphasis on the last part of that sentence: they are *not implemented by man*. In the above passage of Scripture, it states that Christ did not enter the holy place made by the hands of men. This speaks of the tabernacle, which God had instructed the people to build in the wilderness, which was of an earthly and worldly sphere, but rather the spiritual tabernacle in heaven.

Likewise, we read in Hebrews, "But Christ being come an high priest of good things to come, by a greater and more perfect tabernacle, not made with hands, that is to say, not of this building; neither by the blood of goats and calves, but by his own blood he entered in once into the holy place, having obtained eternal redemption for us" (Hebrews 9:11–12). In these two passages of Scripture, the writer reiterates that Jesus Christ entered a spiritual tabernacle, which was not made by man, nor of this creation. In the heavenly tabernacle, Jesus presented His blood as a ransom payment for sin, which would wash away the sin of those who believed by faith.

## Redemption through the Blood

Not only was the tabernacle in which Jesus offered His sacrifice different, but the blood offered was different, too. Jesus, as our High Priest, did not offer the blood of goats or calves as a sin offering to atone for sins. On Calvary's cross, Jesus the Messiah poured out His own blood, which gave Him access as the High Priest into the heavenly Holy of Holies. There, He sprinkled it upon the Mercy Seat. Jesus' blood was unique because in His humanity He was sinless and as to His Person, divine. The blood of Jesus was the only blood pure enough to make atonement for men's sins, and the only blood that God in heaven would accept as a sin offering.

Regarding the ransom payment, in Hebrews, the Bible states, "By his own blood he entered in once into the holy place, having obtained eternal redemption for us" (Hebrews 9:12). Let's define the word *redemption* from the *Vine's Expository Dictionary of Biblical Words*. The Greek word translated "redemption," *lutrosis*, speaks of the redemptive work of Christ bringing deliverance, through His death, from the guilt and power of sin. The verb form of this word means "to release on receipt of ransom; to redeem or liberate by payment of a ransom price." The word *ransom*, from the Greek word *lutron*, was used as the ransom money paid in freeing a slave. All sinners and unbelievers are slaves to sin and Satan. Jesus' sacrifice on the cross paid for our freedom, and the ransom money is His blood. The apostle Peter stated:

## God Provides a Cure for Sin

> Forasmuch as ye know that ye were not redeemed with corruptible things, as silver and gold, from your vain conversation received by tradition from your fathers; but with the precious blood of Christ, as of a lamb without blemish and without spot.
>
> **—1 Peter 1:18–19**

Our redemption cannot be purchased by material things, such as silver, gold, or any other form of currency. Only the blood of Jesus, who offered Himself as a sacrificial Lamb, is without any kind of defects, perfect. As previously stated, all sinners are enslaved to sin and Satan. A person who has never been born again or saved, no matter how many good deeds they may have done, is still a sinner. When the believing sinner repents and confesses his sins to God, believing by faith in what Jesus secured for them on Calvary's cross, he becomes a beneficiary of the ransom paid by the blood of Jesus. Thus, he is purchased, or delivered out of the slave market of sin, becoming the possession of Christ Jesus. The apostle Paul wrote, "For ye are bought with a price: therefore glorify God in your body, and in your spirit, which are God's" (1 Corinthians 6:20).

There are various facets of the work of the blood of Jesus in the life of a new Christian. First, it cleanses and remove sin from the inner man, which consists of the soul and spirit. Remember, it is the spiritual part of man that is saved or delivered. Scripture tells us that Jesus "washed us from our sins in his own blood" (Revelation 1:5). Second, the blood of Jesus removes the guilt of sin from our conscience. Sin had permeated the mental framework of man, whereby every thought and imagination of the heart was evil continuously (see Genesis 6:5). It is written in Hebrews 9:14, "How much more shall the blood of Christ, who through the eternal Spirit offered himself without spot to God, purge our conscience from dead works to serve the living God."

Third, the blood of Jesus removed the penalty of sin. Sin causes spiritual death, simply separation from God and the God kind of life. Scripture says, "The soul that sinneth, it shall die" (Ezekiel 18:4), and "the wages of sin is death" (Romans 6:23). With sin now removed from the inner man, those who are now saved are no longer spiritually dead, but alive in Christ Jesus. Lastly, reconciliation can now take place. Paul wrote, "Much more then, being now justified by his blood, we shall be saved from wrath through him. For if, when we were enemies, we were reconciled to God by the death of his Son, much more, being reconciled, we shall be saved by his life" (Romans 5:9–10). The key word here is *justified*, meaning "to be declared righteous." The person who is declared righteous has been acquitted

## God Provides a Cure for Sin

by the blood of Jesus. Having sins exonerated, and being no longer an enemy, the believer in Christ is reconciled to God, and fellowship is renewed.

In this chapter, we have covered a lot of ground, and there are three key facts you need to remember. These facts are essential for your spiritual growth and victorious life in Christ. First, because Jesus carried our sins in His body on the tree, the body of sin, or the sin nature that lives within our flesh, has been obliterated, rendered powerless. Simply put, the sin nature no longer has power over you; the only power it has is when you give it power by yielding to your flesh. We will discuss mortifying and crucifying the flesh in chapter 9.

Second, the blood of Jesus has cleansed your soul and spirit (your inner man) from all sin. The Bible states, "In whom we have redemption through his blood, the forgiveness of sins, according to the riches of his grace" (Ephesians 1:7). If the removal of sin and the guilt of it is the criterion for mankind to have a relationship with God, what makes us think we can have a relationship with Him and still sin? Keep yourself pure. Lastly, because of the sacrificial death of Jesus and His resurrection, we likewise can experience a new life that is spiritual, created in Christ. This life is eternal. Jesus said, "Verily, verily, I say unto you, he that heareth my word, and believeth on him that sent me, hath everlasting life, and shall not come into condemnation; but is passed from death unto life" (John 5:24). Eternal life begins the moment you accept Jesus Christ as your Savior.

In closing this chapter, I want to take a moment to look back to Calvary's cross. In John 19:31–32, the soldiers began to break the legs of both men who were crucified with Jesus, to accelerate their deaths. When the solders came to Jesus, they saw He was already dead; He had given up the spirit already, so there was no need to break His legs. However, one soldier decided to take his spear and stick it in Jesus' side. Let's read the account: "But one of the soldiers with a spear pierced his side, and forthwith came there out blood and water" (John 19:34). The Scripture states that from this open wound came blood and water. As the blood and water ran down His side, it fell onto the ground and was absorbed into earth. Regarding the blood for our redemption and the water, representing the Word, Jesus said, "Now ye are clean through the word which I have spoken unto you" (John 15:3). Let's fast-forward to the book of 1 John, where it states:

> Who is he that overcometh the world, but he that believeth that Jesus is the Son of God? This is he that came by water and

## God Provides a Cure for Sin

blood, even Jesus Christ, not by water only, but by water and blood. And it is the Spirit that beareth witness, because the Spirit is truth. For there are three that bear record in heaven, the Father, the Word, and the Holy Ghost: and these three are one. And there are three that bear witness in earth, the Spirit, and the water, and the blood and these three agree in one.

**—1 John 5:5–8**

Jesus' blood is still active in the earth today, redeeming mankind and cleansing them of their sins.

# PART 2

*A New Life Experience in Christ*

# PART 2

# CHAPTER 3

## *The Beginning of a New Life Journey*

The *Webster's New College Dictionary* defines *journey* as "any course or passage from one stage or experience to another." Life itself can be defined as a journey, and you have the choice to choose which road you will travel. There are only two choices. The Scriptures speak of a wide and broad road that leads to destruction, and a straight and narrow road that leads to life (Matthew 7:13–14). Every person who ever lives will travel on one of these two roads. Your eternal destination depends on the road you travel. The narrow road leads to eternal life in Christ. The traveler on the wide, broad road, however, will end up in the lake that burns with fire and brimstone (Revelation 20:14–15).

So often today, people say that "life is all about the journey." Simply put, they put credence on what they achieve, experience, and accomplish along the way. But life's accomplishments mean nothing if Jesus Christ is not the focal point of your life. The world's opinion of a successful, prosperous life, and God's view of the same, are quite different. Jesus said, "Take heed, and beware of covetousness: for a man's life consisteth not in the abundance of the things which he possesseth" (Luke 12:15). Earthly possessions will not follow us into eternity. One day, this life journey will come to an end, and everyone will be held accountable for their life choices. The Scripture states, "For we must all appear before the judgment seat of Christ; that every one may receive the things done in his body, according to that he hath done, whether it be good or bad" (2 Corinthians 5:10).

The person who is saved and has given their life to Christ has chosen to travel the narrow road. However, there is an extreme contrast between life on the narrow road and life on the broad road. For example, if you have spent your entire life in the United States, you may have grown familiar with the laws and customs here. Nonetheless, if you relocated to France, you would have to adjust to a completely new set of laws and customs. What may be acceptable in the United States may be a violation in France, because their laws and customs are different. A person cannot adapt to such a radical change of environment and flourish without knowledge of the customs, laws, and language of the land.

Likewise, the earth is comprised of two spiritual kingdoms. This does not mean they are imaginary or philosophical constructs. They are real, but they are not political or geographical kingdoms. Rather, they are worldwide, and they exist in people's souls and spirits. Every person in the world belongs to one of these two kingdoms. You are either a citizen of the kingdom of darkness or the kingdom of God. Everyone and everything in the kingdom of God must be in alignment with God to partake of all God has for His citizens. The same alignment occurs in the kingdom of darkness. In that kingdom, everything and everyone lines up with the devil. By default, we are birth into this kingdom, or sphere of darkness. In chapter 1, we referenced Ephesians 2:2–3, which described the condition of fallen humanity. I stated that we were children of disobedience by choice, as we willingly transgress God's will, and by nature, we were children of wrath, because of Adam's sin, which affected all humanity.

I often say that the spirit world influences everything and everyone. The ways of the kingdom of darkness, the old life, also known as the works of the flesh, include adultery, fornication, uncleanness, witchcraft, lying, murdering, envy, jealousy, hatred, strife, and drunkenness (see Galatians 5:19–21). However, thanks be to God through the Lord Jesus, "who hath delivered us from the power of darkness, and hath translated us into the kingdom of his dear Son" (Colossians 1:13). You have been born into the kingdom of God, which is governed by kingdom principles and kingdom laws. Conformity to the kingdom is a priority, and Jesus must be the Lord of your life.

## The Kingdom of Heaven

During Jesus' ministry, He spent a lot of time talking about the kingdom and the power of the kingdom of God. For example, Jesus said, "But if I cast out devils by the Spirit of God, then the kingdom of God is come unto you" (Matthew 12:28). When defining the *kingdom of God*, we are speaking of the rule of God over all moral intelligence willingly subject to His will, including angels and all believers throughout the ages.

I want to pause a moment to examine two passages of Scripture. The first is in Matthew: "From that time Jesus began to preach, and to say, Repent: for the kingdom of heaven is at hand" (Matthew 4:17). This was a prophetic word as Jesus introduced the coming kingdom. It was not yet here, but its coming was at hand. The next passage is a prayer almost everyone is familiar with or has heard. This prayer is called the Lord's Prayer, and it is found in Matthew 6:9–13. I want to focus on verses 10 through 13, because these petitions would not come to fruition until the death and resurrection of Jesus. Like the words of Matthew 4:17, this prayer was a prophetic prayer. Jesus instructed

His disciples to pray in this way:

> Thy kingdom come, Thy will be done in earth, as it is in heaven. Give us this day our daily bread. And forgive us our debts, as we forgive our debtors. And lead us not into temptation, but deliver us from evil.
>
> **—Matthew 6:10–13**

Let us look at the petitions of this prayer. First, "Thy kingdom come": When Jesus died, He ushered in His kingdom. This kingdom would be within every believer in Christ. Jesus confirmed this when He said, "The kingdom of God is within you" (Luke 17:21). It is a kingdom of light, and its citizens are called children of the light. The Scripture says, "Ye are all the children of light, and the children of the day: we are not of the night, nor of darkness" (1 Thessalonians 5:5). Next, "Thy will be done in earth, as it is in heaven": This kingdom would function as, or mirror things in, the heavenly kingdom, whereby God's will would be done in and through lives of believers as they submit to Him.

"Give us this day our daily bread": Just as the Lord God fed the children of Israel manna—bread from heaven—we also are fed daily bread as the Holy Spirit reveals God's Word to us. Jesus said, "Man shall not live by bread alone, but by every word that proceedeth out of the mouth of God" (Matthew 4:4). "Forgive us our debts": The blood of Jesus has paid the redemption price. When we confess our sins to Him, our sins are forgiven, and we must then learn to forgive others. "Lead us not into temptation": With the Holy Spirit orchestrating the affairs of our lives, we will be victorious over the world, the flesh, and the devil. Like God the Father, and Jesus, the Holy Spirit is holy and "cannot be tempted with evil, neither tempteth he any man" (James 1:13).

Entrance to the kingdom of God is by the new birth. Jesus said, "Except a man be born of water and of the Spirit, he cannot enter into the kingdom of God" (John 3:5). The moment a person confesses and repents of their sins, and by faith believes in what Jesus accomplished on Calvary's cross, they are saved. The apostle Paul wrote:

> That if thou shalt confess with thy mouth the Lord Jesus, and shalt believe in thine heart that God hath raised him from the dead, thou shalt be saved. For with the heart man believeth unto righteousness; and with the mouth confession is made unto salvation. For whosoever shall call upon the name of the Lord shall be saved.
>
> **—Romans 10:9–10, 13**

## The Beginning of a New Life Journey

The Greek translation for the word "saved" is *sozo*, while the Greek translation for "salvation" is *soteria*. Both words imply deliverance. The born-again believer in Christ Jesus is delivered from the power and presence of sin within their soul and spirit. Because their sins have been washed away, they also have been delivered from spiritual death and the influence of the devil. However, there are many garments that must still be taken off, much work yet to be done. The prophet Isaiah wrote these words:

> And a highway will be there; it will be
> called the Way of Holiness; it will be for
> those who walk on that Way. The unclean
> will not journey on it; wicked fools will
> not go about on it.
>
> —**Isaiah 35:8** NIV

One cannot be a traveler on the narrow road or be a kingdom citizen and continue to be governed by the flesh. The task of taking off the garments of the flesh may seem daunting, and you may feel overwhelmed. You have been clothed in them from birth, but do not be discouraged, because you have help in the Person of the Holy Spirit. We will discuss the Holy Spirit work within you in the next chapter.

# CHAPTER 4

## *The Work of the Holy Spirit in the Believer's Life*

Now we come to the Holy Spirit and the role He will play in your Christian life and maturation. Everything needed to sustain you in your spiritual life will come from Him. For man to live up to God's standard, he would need assistance. He must learn to submit to the Holy Spirit so that He can do His work in you and through you. The Lord God said, "I will put my spirit within you, and cause you to walk in my statutes, and ye shall keep my judgments, and do them" (Ezekiel 36:27). Under the influence of the sin nature, man has repeatedly disappointed God. Due to this inherit condition, the apostle Paul wrote, "So then they that are in the flesh cannot please God" (Romans 8:8). Simply put, those who are currently under the influence of the sin nature cannot live a godly life.

In John 14:16–18; 14:26; and 15:26, Jesus said:

> And I will pray the Father, and he shall give you another Comforter, that he may abide with you for ever; even the Spirit of truth; whom the world cannot receive, because it seeth him not, neither knoweth

him: but ye know him; for he dwelleth with you, and shall be in you. I will not leave you comfortless: I will come to you. But the Comforter, which is the Holy Ghost, whom the Father will send in my name, he shall teach you all things, and bring all things to your remembrance, whatsoever I have said unto you. But when the Comforter is come, whom I will send unto you from the Father, even the Spirit of truth, which proceedeth from the Father, he shall testify of me.

Three times in those passages of Scripture, Jesus referred to the Holy Spirit as the "Comforter." The *Vine's Expository Dictionary of Biblical Words* tells us that "comforter" comes from the Greek word *parakletos*, meaning "to call to one's side or to one's aid, it is primarily a verbal adjective, and suggest the capability or adaptability for giving aid or to assist. In the widest sense, it signifies a succorer, comforter." The Holy Spirit's presence within the life of the believer is so vital that the Scripture states, "Now if any man have not the Spirit of Christ, he is none of his" (Romans 8:9). It is impossible to be saved and not have the Holy Spirit. His presence is necessary because there is no spiritual life apart from Him. The Holy Spirit will be with you throughout your Christian life, so it's very important that you do not grieve Him. (See Ephesians 4:30.) I cannot emphasize this enough: He will lead you and guide you as you seek to understand your new life in Christ. Therefore, it is imperative that you die to yourself and submit to His authority, so you can continue to grow spiritually.

The aim is to become Christlike, and only the Holy Spirit has the power to bring you to that point. Throughout this book, I will delve into the many facets of the Holy Spirit's work in the life of the believer. However, for now, let's start with the initial act of salvation and the Holy Spirit baptizing new converts into Jesus Christ.

## The Baptism of the Holy Spirit into Jesus Christ

Throughout Jesus' ministry, He often spoke of the coming Holy Spirit and His baptism. The Holy Spirit baptism was even a focal point of the ministry and teachings of John the Baptist, as stated by him: "John answered, saying unto them all, I indeed baptize you with water; but one mightier than I cometh, the latchet of whose shoes I am not worthy to unloose: he shall baptize you with the Holy Ghost and with fire" (Luke 3:16). Every new convert in Christ will experience the Holy Spirit baptism.

As previously stated in chapter 2, Jesus came to provide

a cure for sin through His sacrificial death and through His blood. Though a cure for sin was now available, there was not a spiritual vehicle in place to immerse believers into all that Jesus had accomplished by His death, burial, and resurrection. That would come fifty days later. The initial baptism of the Holy Spirit took place on the Day of Pentecost. *Pentecost* means "fiftieth day." On that day, the Holy Spirit was poured out and filled those who were present in the Upper Room. Thus, the Holy Spirit became the spiritual conduit to all the benefits made available by our suffering Savior, Jesus Christ.

Before I go further, I want to reiterate that everything concerning salvation, your relationship with God, and your life in Christ takes place in the heavenly or spiritual realm. We worship Him in spirit. There is nothing a person can do of themselves to implement, merit, or acquire it, because it is not a work of man. Only the Holy Spirit can baptize you into Jesus Christ.

The *Vine's Expository Dictionary of Biblical Words* defines "baptism" as coming from the Greek word *baptisma*, meaning an "immersion or placement into something, to submerge." The Holy Spirit's baptizing work emphasizes His bringing believers into a spiritual position in Jesus and into spiritual union with Jesus Christ and other believers.

## The Work of the Holy Spirit in the Believer's Life

The Scripture states in Galatians:

> For as many of you as have been baptized into Christ have put on Christ. There is neither Jew nor Greek, there is neither bond nor free, there is neither male nor female: for ye are all one in Christ Jesus.
>
> **—Galatians 3:27–28**

I would like to pause here for a moment to explain being baptized into Christ. The moment a person confesses their sins and repents with godly sorrow, immediately the Holy Spirit comes, takes their soul and spirit, and immerses it into Jesus Christ. For more clarity, let us examine a passage of Scripture in the book of Romans:

> Know ye not, that so many of us as were baptized into Jesus Christ were baptized into his death? Therefore we are buried with him by baptism into death: that like as Christ was raised up from the dead by the glory of the Father, even so we also should walk in newness of life.
>
> **—Romans 6:3–4**

"Baptism" here is not referring to your pastor or the deacon of your church immersing you in a pool or lake. The ritual of water baptism is a symbolic reenactment of the believer's participation in Jesus' death, burial, and resurrection by virtue of his spiritual union with Him. Simply put, it represents an outward sign of an inner change. However, if the person who is being baptized has never been born again of the Holy Spirit, water baptism cannot and will not change them nor will it change their relationship with God; they are still sinners. Sadly, more emphasis is often placed on water baptism than on the baptism of the Holy Spirit into the body of Christ. In the gospel of Luke, we see a paradigm shift concerning baptisms. The shifting is from a water baptism to the baptism of the Holy Spirit. The Scripture confirms this in Luke:

> Now when all the people were baptized, it came to pass, that Jesus also being baptized, and praying, the heaven was opened, and the Holy Ghost descended in a bodily shape like a dove upon him, and a voice came from heaven, which said, Thou art my beloved Son; in thee I am well pleased.
>
> —**Luke 3:21–22**

Prior to Pentecost, Jesus was the only Person to have experienced the baptism of the Holy Spirit. Simply put, He was filled full within His inner man. This shifting ushered in a new and living way God would deal with mankind. Only the Holy Spirit could produce spiritual life as He quickens the inner man. Again, it is not the physical

### The Work of the Holy Spirit in the Believer's Life

man that's being saved, but it is the inner man, our soul and spirit. Remember, Jesus is the pattern; as it happened with Him, so must it happen with us. The Holy Spirit's baptism placed us into Jesus, and His indwelling brought Jesus into us.

Referring back to Romans 6:3–4, Paul said those who are baptized into Christ were baptized into His death. When the Holy Spirit immersed your soul and spirit into Christ, at that moment, your sins were washed away by His blood, and the sin nature that resides in the flesh was rendered powerless. Due to Jesus' bearing our sins in His own body, the body of sin has been destroyed. We became beneficiaries of all that Jesus accomplished and fulfilled on the cross. This baptism of the Holy Spirit brought forth regeneration. Regeneration is an act of God, the Holy Spirit, whereby in response to saving faith, He cleanses and renews the believer's soul and spirit and imparts spiritual life. The Scripture explains in Titus: "Not by works of righteousness which we have done, but according to his mercy he saved us, by the washing of regeneration, and renewing of the Holy Ghost" (Titus 3:5). This renewing work of regeneration is preceded by cleansing, or the removal of guilt and defilement caused by sin.

Paul further added that we were buried with him by baptism into death. This signified a radical spiritual change in the believer's life as the old man and his sinful nature has been obliterated. Just as Christ was raised from the dead, by the glory of the Father, likewise we are raised from the death that was caused by sin, to a newness of life in Christ Jesus. Paul continues his discourse by saying:

> For if we have been planted together in the likeness of his death, we shall be also in the likeness of his resurrection: knowing this, that our old man is crucified with him, that the body of sin might be destroyed, that henceforth we should not serve sin. For he that is dead is free from sin.
>
> **—Romans 6:5–7**

This Holy Spirit baptism has brought the believer into oneness with Christ. This oneness is with your inner man (see Ephesians 3:16). Thus, being infused or planted together in the likeness of His death, we also shall be in the likeness of His resurrection. A new spiritual life in Christ begins. We are new creations in Christ Jesus, and the old manner of living is now behind us. A new spiritual life commences, and all things are now new. Now being born again in Christ, we are sealed with the Holy Spirit of promise (see Ephesians 1:13).

The sealing of the Holy Spirit is the work of God the

Father, who sets the Holy Spirit as a seal upon every believer, to preserve him until the redemption of his body, which completes his salvation. The word *sealed* means "to set a seal upon," or "to mark with a seal." A seal is a device with a design that can impart an impression onto a soft substance. In the Bible, a seal signifies several things, of which I would like to address two: ownership and security.

Regarding divine ownership, every Christian has been purchased out of the slave market of sin by the blood of Jesus. Thus, you are now God's property, a purchased possession, and your body is His temple, or dwelling place. The life we now live should be lived to the glory of God. Simply put, God should get the glory in everything we do and speak. The Lord knows all those who belong to Him. Jesus said, "My sheep hear my voice, and I know them, and they follow me: And I give unto them eternal life; and they shall never perish, neither shall any man pluck them out of my hand. My Father, which gave them me, is greater than all; and no man is able to pluck them out of my Father's hand" (John 10:27–29). In 2 Timothy Paul wrote, "Nevertheless the foundation of God standeth sure, having this seal, The Lord knoweth them that are his. And, let every one that nameth the name of Christ depart from iniquity" (2 Timothy 2:19). The Holy Spirit is the seal of ownership that we obtain at salvation. Every believer has been bought with the blood of Jesus; therefore, we are a purchased possession unto Him. Being citizens of His kingdom, we must depart from iniquity. Just as our Lord and Savior is holy, we must be holy also.

Regarding divine security and protection, we are sealed with the Holy Spirit of promise. The Holy Spirit will be with us throughout the journey of life as He navigates us through this barren, wicked, dark world. The main significance of the Holy Spirit's sealing seems to be security. In Revelation 7:2–3, it is written, "And I saw another angel ascending from the east, having the seal of the living God: and he cried with a loud voice to the four angels, to whom it was given to hurt the earth and the sea, Saying, Hurt not the earth, neither the sea, nor the trees, till we have sealed the servants of our God in their foreheads." That passage of Scripture refers to the sealing of the one hundred and forty-four thousand Jews who would evangelize the earth in seven years, twelve thousand from each of the twelve tribes of Israel. Paul wrote to the church at Ephesus: "And grieve not the holy Spirit of God, whereby ye are sealed unto the day of redemption" (Ephesians 4:30). The Holy Spirit was sent to aid us in our Christian life, and He will keep us if we are willing to be kept. As you journey through life, always remember, "The Lord is faithful, who shall stablish you, and keep you from evil" (2 Thessalonians 3:3).

## The Work of the Holy Spirit in the Believer's Life

As I close this chapter, we must remember that although our fleshly body still has the sin force in it, sin is no longer the motivating influence in our life. However, our saved inner man is still susceptible to the sin force that is resident in the flesh if we submit to it. Knowledge is powerful, and knowing that the Lord has His seal upon us, and that He is able to protect us and keep us during times of testing, is powerful. "Now unto him that is able to keep you from falling, and to present you faultless before the presence of his glory with exceeding joy" (Jude 24). Let's continue to press forward toward the mark of the prize in Christ Jesus.

# CHAPTER 5

## *Empowered to Live*

Everything I have covered thus far detailing the life we have been saved to live may seem a bit ovewhelming. The moment you had your initial God-encounter and were saved, some of the desires of the old man or sin nature, the Lord immediately removed from you. As I reflect on my salvation experience, I recall things I instantly no longer desired to do; however, there was so much I had to intentionally walk away from and mortify in my flesh. The next statement I am going to make I hope resonates throughout your soul and spirit: *You do not have to commit acts of sin!* It doesn't matter what you may think, believe, say, or even what you may hear on some religious programs, and from some pulpits, the fact is you *can* live a holy, righteous life. The Scriptures teach that you can, and that should be the precedent in your life, not the idea that you can't.

Sadly, we have been indoctrinated by religious groups and unsaved individuals to believe that living a holy righteous life is impossible while in this body on the earth. Thus, we have the absence of the word *sin* from many of the messages you hear on Sunday or midweek. However, you will hear the word *mistakes* quite often, which is used instead of the word *sin* to appease people. From our pulpits, we hear statements such as, "You're going to make mistakes along the way." Simply put, what they are attempting to say is that you will occasionally sin. Well, the Word of God never told us that, nor does it encourage us to sin after we been saved. Furthermore, the word *mistake* is not found written anywhere in Scripture. Because of this, you hear many in the church say that "we are not perfect," or "we are going to make mistakes," in order to justify acts of sin they are committing. If you believe you are going to sin, you will.

We must rise to a higher spiritual standard and begin to view life through the lens of God's Word, allowing God through the Holy Spirit to change the way we think. The Scripture says, "For as he thinketh in his heart, so is he" (Proverbs 23:7). Your thoughts, if mediated upon long enough, will become woven into the fabric of your soul and spirit. Simply put, if you believe it's impossible to live a holy life, you will not. Keep in mind what Jesus accomplished for us on the cross: every believer's sin has been washed away. We are no longer enslaved by the sin force that resides within our flesh. God would never require His people to do something that's impossible to achieve. Our Lord has supplied us with everything needed to live a holy,

## Empowered to Live

Christlike life. You have been divinely empowered to live! Jesus said, "But ye shall receive power, after that the Holy Ghost is come upon you" (Acts 1:8).

When reading Acts 1:8, the first thought that comes to mind is "divine empowerment to do kingdom work," such as healing the sick, casting out evil spirits, operating in the spiritual gifts, preaching the Gospel, and so on. We have become so enamored with these things, and we should be when God's power is manifested in our presence. However, the scope of His power does not end there. The Greek word for "power" in Acts 1:8 is *dunamis*, which implies "strength, power, and ability." We are given power to perform miracles, and we receive moral power and excellence of soul. When reading Acts 1:8, we rarely think of divine empowerment to live a Christian life. The greatest evidence of a changed life or a born-again experience is how you live before men. People who know you will be watching to see if your life measures up to what you believe and confess. Paul wrote to the Church:

> Ye are our epistle written in our hearts, known and read of all men: Forasmuch as ye are manifestly declared to be the epistle of Christ ministered by us, written not with ink, but with the Spirit of the living God.
>
> **—2 Corinthians 3:2–3**

### Now That I Have Been Born Again, *What's Next?*

Every born-again believer's life is a book that is read daily by those whom we encounter. Sadly, many who confess to be Christians are not good witnesses due to the lives they live. We can't drink, party, use profanity, and sin with unbelievers and then invite them to church or attempt to lead them to Christ. They may not see the need to go to church or accept Jesus as Lord because they see you living and doing the same things they are doing. God is all about changing your life. You can't implement change yourself, but God, through the power of the Holy Spirit, has empowered you to live a holy, consecrated life. Everything needed to successfully live a Christlike life has been given to us. We must understand that positionally we are now in Christ; thus, we inherit His virtues.

In the book of Colossians, the apostle Paul further explains how the believer is positionally in Christ and we have been divinely empowered to live the Christian life. The Scriptures declare, "For in him dwelleth all the fulness of the Godhead bodily. And ye are complete in him, which is the head of all principality and power" (Colossians 2:9–10).

Before we begin unpacking the various golden nuggets within those two passages of Scripture—and there's a lot to unpack—I want to take a moment to again stress this thought: God the Father, God the Son, and God the Holy Spirit are holy, pure, and sinless. Every Christian is seated in Christ Jesus, and has the Holy Spirit dwelling within them; therefore, we should live as Jesus lived (see 1 John 2:6). Remember, no matter what anyone says, committing an act of sin is a choice, and no longer a way of life, for the believer in Christ. We have been given power to overcome; therefore, we should not yield to the evil desires of our flesh. We must choose to walk in obedience because we love God and desire to remain in fellowship with our Savior.

Referring to Colossians 2:9–10, I would like to define for clarity the words *dwelleth, fullness*, and *complete*, found in the ninth and tenth verses, according to *Vine's Expository Dictionary of Biblical Words*. The ninth verse opens by stating, "In Him," referring to Jesus Christ, "dwelleth." "Dwelleth," from the Greek word *katoikeo*, means "to live, to dwell fixedly in a place." This word speaks of permanence. The fullness of the Godhead is and was continuously active and permanently residing within Jesus. Simply put, the total essence of God and who God is was in Jesus while on earth, as well after His ascension. Fullness is *pleroma*, referring to all His virtues and excellencies. The totality of divine powers and attributes of God, and who God is, are permanently in Jesus. Paul declares that in the

Son dwells all the fullness of the absolute Godhead.

Paul continues his discourse by stating that every believer is complete in Him, Christ. The Greek word for "complete" is *pleroo*, meaning "to be made full." Literally, you are in Christ, having been filled full, with the present result being that the believer of Christ is in a state of fullness. Just as we are holy because Christ is holy, and just as our righteousness comes from His righteousness, our fullness comes from His fullness. His fullness is transfused into you, the believer, by virtue of your baptism into Him. Therefore, the Church, the body of Christ, is regarded as the fullness of Christ because all His graces and energies are communicated to her. In the Ephesian letter, the apostle Paul stated that "we are His workmanship created in Christ Jesus" (Ephesians 2:10). "Created" here is the word *ktizo*, the Greek equivalent to the Hebrew *bara*, meaning "to create," and it is used exclusively of God's creative activity. The born-again believer is created in Christ, with His virtues, and totally filled full of everything needed to live a Christ-centered life. Let that sink in a moment. You have been divinely empowered to live! Peter also confirms this fact in his writings:

> According as his divine power hath given unto us all things that pertain unto life and godliness, through the knowledge of

> him that hath called us to glory and virtue: Whereby are given unto us exceeding great and precious promises: that by these ye might be partakers of the divine nature, having escaped the corruption that is in the world through lust.
>
> —2 Peter 1:3–4

Throughout the New Testament, the message is clear that God has empowered us and equipped us with everything needed to live the Christian life. God is the Source of all power, and we are depending on His power and presence residing within us to sustain us. Peter further added that we are partakers of His divine nature. This divine nature, implanted in the inner being of the believing sinner, becomes the source of our new life and actions. The divine nature gives the believer both the desire and the power to do God's will. The word *divine* speaks of the attributes of God, or of God seen from the standpoint of His attributes. Becoming a partaker of the divine nature does not mean you will partake of the attributes of deity, such as omnipotence, omnipresence, and omniscience, which are incommunicable. However, many of His attributes and virtues, like holiness, love, and righteousness, *are* communicated to the inner man, the soul and spirit, at the point of salvation.

Power again is *dunamis,* inherent power, power that overcomes resistance, power residing in a thing by virtue of its nature. Through God's divine power, He has bestowed upon every Christian all things that pertain to life and godliness. "Life" is *zoe*; this word is used to designate the life God gives to the believing sinner, a spiritual life hidden in Christ. As I stated earlier, God is all about change, transforming us from sinners to saints, and only He has the power to bring forth change in the core of our being.

Christians are endowed with a new nature, and we are capable, through God's mercy, of acquiring the moral character of our divine Creator. Now fashioned in the likeness of God, man, under the Holy Spirit's influence, can walk in love, righteousness, and holiness. You have been divinely empowered to live a Christlike life. God's presence will always abide within you in the person of the Holy Spirit and the engrafted Word. No one said it would be easy; in fact, Jesus Himself said, "If any man will come after me, let him deny himself, and take up his cross, and follow me" (Matthew 16:24). At the point of salvation, God has deposited within the spirit of man all things needed to live a holy life, but the intellectual framework of man (the soul and the mind) must be renewed in knowledge. The sin nature is currently still active within our flesh, but we no longer are enslaved to it, nor must we yield to it. Our strength and faith are in the Lord, knowing that greater is He that is in us and we now can overcome the spirit of the world. We have been empowered by God to live a Christlike life, so let the growth process begin!

# PART III

*Growing in the Grace and
Knowledge of God*

# CHAPTER 6

## *Newborn Babies in Christ*

As newborn babes, desire the sincere milk of the word, that ye may grow thereby.

**—1 Peter 2:2**

Salvation occurs the moment a person accepts Jesus as Lord, but sanctification is a lifelong process. God uses His Word to sanctify believers. Jesus said, "Sanctify them through thy truth: thy word is truth" (John 17:17). The truth of the Gospel cleanses us and set us apart for His service. As we seek instruction from the Scriptures, we must trust the Holy Spirit to provide revelation and understanding.

In many cases, the new convert, or born-again believer, has no idea of the spiritual life ahead of them and how the process of sanctification occurs. Having this knowledge will be very beneficial as your new life in Christ begins. You have been birthed into God's kingdom and family. It does not matter how young or old you are, as a saved, born-again believer, you are a baby in Christ. A baby is extremely vulnerable and needs to be natured and protected. Thus, the first six to twelve months of your new life in Christ is very important, as you will either begin to grow spiritually or become stagnant and revert to serving the flesh.

Unknowingly, you have entered a spiritual war, and many of your friends and even some family members may criticize your decision to become a follower of Christ. Then there is the enemy of your soul, the devil, who will be in full "attack mode" because of your decision to abandon him for Christ.

In the above passage of Scripture, the apostle Paul described new converts as "newborn babes." The recipients of this letter are considered "just-born infants" in their spiritual walk. In the natural world, a newborn is dependent on their parents to feed, nurture, and protect them. Moreover, the parents are responsible for the social and moral advancement of that child until it reaches maturity, or adulthood.

I would like to address three words before we proceed. In the previous paragraph, I mentioned that a newborn infant in Christ is vulnerable and needs to be nurtured and protected. Let's first define *protected* and *vulnerable*. To *protect* means "to shield from injury, danger, or loss; to guard and defend." In defining the word *vulnerable*, the *Webster's New College Dictionary* states that it means "open to attack; easily hurt as by adverse criticism; sensitive; can be wounded; affected by a specified influence, and temptation."

In the introduction of this book, I mentioned the importance of growing wherever God planted you. You may not know people at the church where you were saved, but God has planted you there for a reason. If you have plants, you will be able to relate to this illustration. You can have a plant that is thriving in its original pot and soil. Then, due to the growth of the plant, you decide to replant it. So, you go and purchase a bigger pot and additional soil and repot the plant therein. However, the plant does not thrive and grow as it did in the previous soil and pot. You become frustrated and begin to question what went wrong. It is the same plant—the only difference is the soil and the pot. In many instances, the soil and the pot can influence the continual growth and health of a plant. Likewise, where you worship on Sunday morning can and will have a strong influence on your spiritual life. Friends and family members may want you to fellowship with them at their church, but if that's not where God planted you, then you should decline.

In the gospel of John, Jesus taught about the shepherd and a hireling. He said, "I am the good shepherd: the good shepherd giveth his life for the sheep. But he that is an hireling, and not the shepherd, whose own the sheep are not, seeth the wolf coming, and leaveth the sheep, and fleeth: and the wolf catcheth them, and scattereth the sheep. The hireling fleeth, because he is an hireling, and careth not for the sheep" (John 10:11–13). God has planted you in a place where the under-shepherd, your pastor, will watch over you, encourage you, and protect you during this vulnerable stage of your spiritual infancy. That's his charge, his duty—he is to protect and care for those whom God has entrusted to him. Hirelings are not concerned about your soul, nor your spiritual growth. Hirelings are in it for the money; therefore, when the wolf comes, and you need the protection of a shepherd, he abandons you, because he is just a hireling.

The word *nurtured* is defined as "one that nourishes; feed; the act or process of raising or promoting the development, training, educating, and fostering; the environmental factors collectively, to which one is subjected from conception onward." As spiritual newborns, we must be mindful or careful of whom we allow to feed us spiritually or sow into our souls and spirits. The apostle Paul admonished the elders at Ephesus to feed the Church; as the Scripture proclaims, "Take heed therefore unto yourselves, and to all the flock, over the which the Holy Ghost hath made you overseers, to feed the church of God, which he hath purchased with his own blood" (Acts 20:28). The apostle Peter gave the same message to the elders with whom he was speaking, saying, "Feed the flock of God which is among you" (1 Peter 5:2). It is an absolute necessity that spiritual babies continually hear and receive the truth of the Gospel.

Your relationship with God is built on knowledge. Paul, in writing to the saints at Colossae, said, "Put on the new man, which is renewed in knowledge after the image of him that created him" (Colossians 3:10). That takes us back to 1 Peter 2:2, quoted at the opening of this chapter. In this passage of Scripture, Peter used the birth of an infant child as a metaphor for the life of a newborn Christian. A newborn in the natural has a strong desire for milk or baby formula. This milk or formula is a necessity for that infant's growth. It's important to note that newborns cannot feed themselves; they need someone to feed them. If not fed, the infant child would die of starvation. The nutrients in the milk or formula allow the child to grow in strength and stature as it progresses to the next stage of life, which is that of a young child.

Those to whom Peter is writing this letter are called "just-born infants," speaking of how recent was their new birth into the Christian life. The Greek word translated "desire" speaks of an intense yearning. Newborn infants in Christ are exhorted to have an intense yearning for the pure, unadulterated Word of God. The Word of God nourishes the soul. It has no ulterior motives, like so many teachings of men do. Speaking of the milk (the Word) being unadulterated, we are speaking of the quality of this milk (the Word). The word *milk* here is not speaking of a certain portion of God's Word, but of the Word of God in general. A healthy spiritual baby yearns for God's Word.

However, a natural infant has the tendency to become attached to the person who is feeding them. In the spiritual dynamic, this can become very dangerous, especially when a person establishes a dependency on their pastor or teacher for spiritual feeding and growth instead of on God. Their conversations will reflect this dependency, because when referring to biblical topics, their response will often be, "My pastor said," or "Bishop said," instead referencing the Holy Scriptures. Furthermore, there must come a time in your spiritual growth that you ween yourself from men and trust the Holy Spirit to speak into your life on a personal level.

The word *reveal* means "to uncover, unveil." Simply put, this means "to make known or present to the mind directly." Let's consider some Scripture that relate to this topic.

> But the anointing which ye have received of him abideth in you, and ye need not that any man teach you: but as the same anointing teacheth you of all things, and is truth, and is no lie, and even as it hath taught you, ye shall abide in him.
>
> **—1 John 2:27**

> But God hath revealed them unto us by his Spirit: for the Spirit searcheth all things, yea, the deep things of God.
>
> **—1 Corinthians 2:10**

The Bible is a living spiritual book, and only God the Holy Spirit can truly make it known to us. You can sit under the greatest teacher in the world, but if God does not give you revelation and understanding, you will not comprehend what the Scriptures are saying. If God the Holy Spirit has taken up refuge within you, however, there is no need to be taught by men, because the anointing will teach you everything you need to know to become Christlike, and He teaches truth. You will learn more in your quiet time and daily devotions with the Holy Spirit than you will ever learn in a church building. Having the mind of God, the Holy Spirit knows the deep things of God, and He wants to reveal them to us. Therefore, we must establish a true relationship with God the Holy Spirit, who is able to truly feed us and engraft God's Word within our hearts. This is when transformation really begins. I am not saying you shouldn't go to church; I am stressing the importance of daily having a set time for fellowship with the Lord at home. What would happen if you only fed your body once or twice a week? You would become weak and brittle. Well, the same would happen to your spirit if it was not fed daily. Your spirit needs to be fed for it to grow.

Again, for the preached Word to be effective, it cannot be watered down or diluted; thus we see the significance of the person who is feeding you. In Paul's letter to the church at Ephesus, he speaks of those who have been called into the fivefold ministry and their duty to the body of Christ.

> And he gave some, apostles; and some, prophets; and some, evangelists; and some, pastors and teachers; for the perfecting of the saints, for the work of the ministry, for the edifying of the body of Christ: till we all come in the unity of the faith, and of the knowledge of the Son of God, unto a perfect man, unto the measure of the stature of the fulness of Christ: That we henceforth be no more children, tossed to and fro, and carried about with every wind of doctrine, by the sleight of men, and cunning craftiness, whereby they lie in wait to deceive.
>
> **—Ephesians 4:11–14**

These gifted people are given as a gift to the Church. They specialize in equipping the saints for ministering work—that is, Christian service, saving lost souls, and building up the saints. This can only be accomplished by teaching the truth. Those who are appointed by God to function in these offices are to give instructions concerning Christian living and not to entertain the people. Honestly, I feel the problem with today's churches is that we have strayed from the main doctrines of the Church, such as holiness, sanctification, and righteousness. Thus, we see so much sin within the body. In many cases, sin is not addressed because leaders do not want to offend anyone by speaking the truth. Have we forgotten that the Scriptures are for reproof, correction, and instruction in righteousness?

Today, men desire the gifting, but they do not want the persecution that comes with ministering truth, so they compromise the Word for popularity and personal gain. The early saints were beaten with rods, scourged, beheaded, stoned, and sawn asunder for the Gospel (see Hebrews 11:31-40). However, that did not stop them from ministering the truth, with the results being souls converted to Christ and the saints strengthened. Keep in mind, the aim is to become Christlike and put sin out of our lives. It will be a process; however, the key will be the early training you receive and the biblical foundation you are building upon as you grow.

# CHAPTER 7

## *Child Training*

Train up a child in the way he should go:
and when he is old, he will not depart from it.

**—Proverbs 22:6**

Oftentimes, when this passage of Scripture is read or quoted, immediately we think of training a child from a physical perspective. As the infant grows into childhood and begins to develop self-awareness, and as they reach early adolescence and mature into middle adolescence, the child needs to learn what is acceptable behavior and what is not. One of the first life lessons parents teach their children is how to use the bathroom. This helps improve self-esteem and confidence as they begin to grow. On occasions during the training process, chastisement is used to reinforce the importance of *not* doing something. For example, during my childhood, they didn't have devices to child-proof a home, keeping dangerous items away from investigating, curious minds as we crawled around on the floor or took those first steps. Like all children, I needed instruction. Therefore, my parents would often slap my hands and say "no" when I would reach for the stove or the wall sockets. It was their way of training and teaching me that these items had the potential to harm me.

Everything in life is a learned behavior. A child is born into this world with no knowledge of the life ahead of them. A child learns to talk, walk, and discover what they should abstain from and what is required to be successful. Parents play an important role in character building and influencing the development of their children. Likewise, your pastor will and should play a significant role in your spiritual growth. Again, I stressed in the introduction the importance of the person who is sowing into your spiritual life, the one who is feeding you the Word of God. Is your leader shepherding you, or is he just a hireling with no true concern about your spiritual development? I often say that we are what our parents were because children have a tendency to emulate their fathers and mothers. Consequently, your pastor, bishop, teacher, evangelist, or apostle will leave an imprint on your spiritual life. The strength of your life is the core values that are instilled within you by your parents when you are a child.

So it is also with the Christian life. The newborn Christian is not yet Christlike in their ways, but as the child begin to learn of Him, he will begin to emulate his Savior. As

## Child Training

I stated in chapter 5, the first six months to a year after salvation is important to the newborn in Christ Jesus. During this period, the "child" needs training and instruction as they begin to grow and become more Christlike.

Growth happens in increments, depending on how much knowledge of the Scriptures you obtain. Are you receiving and hearing sound doctrine that will transform your life? The Word of God must become a living *rhema* word engrafted within the soul and spirit, producing an inward change.

I do not want to seem repetitious, but the moment we confess, repent of our sins, and invite the Lord in our hearts, we are saved. However, sanctification is a lifelong process. It doesn't happen overnight. Sanctification is the process of being set apart or set aside for God's purpose. We have been saved to a life of separation. Paul, writing to the church at Corinth, said, "Be ye not unequally yoked together with unbelievers: for what fellowship hath righteousness with unrighteousness? And what communion hath light with darkness? Wherefore come out from among them, and be ye separate, saith the Lord, and touch not the unclean thing; and I will receive you" (2 Corinthians 6:14, 17). If you continue to fraternize with the unsaved, they could have a negative influence on your new life in

Christ. The truth of God's Word not only sanctifies us, but it also cleanses us and produces faith, knowledge, and discipline, which is imperative at this stage of your life. You are building a foundation that will last throughout your Christian life and into eternity.

In the book of Hebrews, the writer wrote several passages of Scripture detailing the training of spiritual children. I am going to quote from the Amplified Bible here for clarity:

> And you have forgotten the divine word of encouragement which is addressed to you as sons, "MY SON, DO NOT MAKE LIGHT OF THE DISCIPLINE OF THE LORD AND DO NOT LOSE HEART and GIVE UP WHEN YOU ARE CORRECTED BY HIM; FOR THE LORD DISCIPLINES and CORRECTS THOSE WHOM HE LOVES, AND HE PUNISHES EVERY SON WHOM HE RECEIVES and WELCOMES [TO HIS HEART]." You must submit to [correction for the purpose of] discipline; God is dealing with you as with sons; for what son is there whom his father does not discipline? Now if you are exempt from correction and without discipline, in which all [of God's children] share, then you are illegitimate children and not sons [at all]. Moreover, we have

had earthly fathers who disciplined us, and we submitted and respected them [for training us]; shall we not much more willingly submit to the Father of spirits, and live [by learning from His discipline]? For our earthly fathers disciplined us for only a short time as seemed best to them; but He disciplines us for our good, so that we may share His holiness. For the time being no discipline brings joy, but seems sad and painful; yet to those who have been trained by it, afterwards it yields the peaceful fruit of righteousness [right standing with God and a lifestyle and attitude that seeks conformity to God's will and purpose].

—Hebrews 12:5–11 AMP

I believe many of the struggles young Christians have overcoming the sin nature can be prevented. Prevention begins at childhood, as the young Christian received instruction and fundamental training in biblical truth. Holiness, righteousness, and sanctification must be instilled within them while they are babies, toddlers, and as young children in Christ. If these spiritual values are instilled within their souls and spirits while they are children, as they grow on to maturity, they will not depart from them. However, if the proper spiritual values are not instilled, then the struggle with the sin nature, or even a particular act of sin, will become a stronghold.

The text above reveals to us that God believes in child training. He trains us because we are His children and because He loves us. As believers of Christ, living in the light, we cannot continue to live the same sinful lifestyle we once lived while in darkness. The King James Version of this text uses the word *chasteneth*; this word speaks of the training and education of children in the things of God and the God kind of life. It speaks also of instruction that aims at the increase of virtue, correcting mistakes and curbing sinful passions. The word *chastening* does not have in it the idea of punishment, but rather, of corrective measures that will eliminate evil in the life of the believer. If God never chastised you, or if you are exempt from chastisement, then you are an illegitimate child and not a son or daughter of the Father. As a son or daughter, God wants the best for you. He wants you to experience the position of sonship and the benefits that come with it. However, to experience the abundant life, your acts of sin must cease.

So often in the child training process, we feel convicted when we do something wrong or when we read a passage of Scripture that challenges us to forsake something. Simply put, that's God's way of training us and revealing to us that we need to stop whatever it may be. If we endure chastisement, God sees us as a son or daughter. Remember, as a loving Father, He knows what is best for us and what's needed to please Him. We are trained and disciplined so that we can become partakers of His holiness. How does this discipline occur?

## Becoming Disciplined in Christ

*Discipline* is defined as "training that develops self-control, character, and orderly conduct, meaning obedience." God is seeking people who would willingly keep covenant and live in obedience to His Word. We must learn to be Christians. That is why the Scripture places a strong emphasis on studying and learning of Him. Jesus said, "Take my yoke upon you, and learn of me" (Matthew 11:29). We must also learn obedience as Jesus did. The Scripture says that Jesus "learned obedience by the things which he suffered" (Hebrews 5:8).

In speaking of self-control, we are referring to the ability to control one's feelings and emotions and to overcome one's weakness. It is the ability to continue to live a righteous life despite the temptations that may confront you. The apostle Paul said to the saints of the church of the Thessalonians, "For this is the will of God, even your sanctification, that ye should abstain from fornication: That every one of you should know how to possess his vessel in sanctification and honour" (1 Thessalonians 4:3–4). Simply put, he was saying that we as saints should be able to control the sinful desires that reside in our fleshly body.

It is very important that we do not lose sight of the fact that sanctification and becoming disciplined is a lifelong process of absolute surrender and obedience to the Word of God. You may lose some skirmishes, but if you stay the course, you will win the war, so be encouraged. God uses the Scriptures to discipline us, to mold our character, and to bring us to a life of obedience. I often say that we can't effectively live a life that we don't have knowledge of or understand. In the gospel of John, Jesus was speaking to some of His Jewish followers, and He said, "If ye continue in my word, then are ye my disciples indeed; and ye shall know the truth, and the truth shall make you free" (John 8:31–32).

A true disciple has become disciplined in the things of God. How did they get to this place in Christ? By daily applying the principles of the Word of God to their lives. Hearing God's Word and applying it are two different things. Paul shared that a day would come when people would be "ever learning, and never able to come to the knowledge of the truth" (2 Timothy 3:7). A rebellious spirit will prevent people from receiving truth even though they have heard it. Therefore, they never obtain spiritual liberty, nor do they arrive at the point of practical application whereby they begin to live by what they have received. We will discuss practical applications in chapter 11. When we hear and receive the Word of God, we will know the truth—not man's version of truth, but God's truth, which liberates. There must be a continuance in God's Word daily—walking in it, abiding in it, and becoming doers of it, and not simply hearers. As James wrote in his epistle:

> But be ye doers of the word, and not
> hearers only, deceiving your own selves.
> For if any be a hearer of the word, and not
> a doer, he is like unto a man beholding his
> natural face in a glass: for he beholdeth
> himself, and goeth his way, and straight-
> way forgetteth what manner of man he
> was. But whoso looketh into the perfect
> law of liberty, and continueth therein, he
> being not a forgetful hearer, but a doer of
> the work, this man shall be blessed in his
> deed.
>
> **—James 1:22–25**

Obedience to the Word of God will bring us to a point of spiritual maturity. First, the Holy Spirit must engraft the received Word within the heart, meaning the soul. The word *engrafted* used in the above passage of Scripture means "to implant, or implanted." The idea is that of a seed rooting itself in the heart, then germinating and producing life. It has cleansing properties. Jesus said, "Ye are clean through the word which I have spoken unto you" (John 15:3). The Bible is an instruction manual. It tells how to live and what we should forsake. Again, we must be doers of the Word and not just hearers. James goes on to explain that the Word of God is a mirror that will give us a true reflection of who we are.

The Word will reveal things in our lives that we need to let go of or walk away from. At that point, it's up to you to surrender your will and mortify that area of your life. However, when a person is not willing to change, they walk away from the Word, forgetting what manner of man or woman they really are. It's easy to justify something that you are not ready to stop doing. Thus, they will tune out that portion of Scripture. The path to being a true disciple and living in spiritual liberty is receiving the truth of God's engrafted Word and conforming to it. Change is always difficult, especially as one has become accustomed to a certain way of life; transitioning your life is never easy, but the rewards are eternal.

# CHAPTER 8

## *A Life in Transition*

One of the biggest challenges you will experience as a newborn infant in Christ will be transitioning your life. *Transition* is defined in the *Webster's New College Dictionary* as a "passing from one condition, form, stage, place, to another." Transition is the period of such passing. You know you have experienced an encounter with God that has changed your life. Your inner being has been awakened and made spiritually alive, but because you are still a spiritual baby, you know nothing about this new life. The Bible says that you have been "delivered from the power of darkness, and translated into the kingdom of his dear Son" (Colossians 1:13). You know all about the past life of darkness from which you were delivered, but you have no knowledge of the kingdom of God, nor the ways of the kingdom.

Solomon wrote, "The thing that hath been, it is that which shall be; and that which is done is that which shall be done: and there is no new thing under the sun" (Ecclesiastes 1:9). The Church, the body of Christ, is not the first group of people whom God has delivered from darkness. He delivered Israel from Egypt and the tyranny of Pharaoh. However, Israel failed miserably when it came to transitioning into a life of liberty. The apostle Paul alludes to the history of the Hebrew people to give warning to the church in 1 Corinthians. Let's begin with 1 Corinthians 10:5–6 and 11:

> But with many of them God was not well pleased: for they were overthrown in the wilderness. Now these things were our examples, to the intent we should not lust after evil things, as they also lusted.
>
> **—1 Corinthians 10:5–6**
>
> Now all these things happened unto them for examples: and they are written for our admonition, upon whom the ends of the world are come.
>
> **—verse 11**

In the previous passages of Scripture that led up to the sixth verse, Paul wrote of the flight of the Hebrew people out of Egypt. He described this supernatural, miraculous event as a "baptism," as they were under the cloud, they all passed through the sea, and they were all baptized unto Moses in the cloud and in the sea. With Pharaoh's army behind them and the Red Sea in front of them, the people began to murmur and complain to Moses (see Exodus 14).

## A Life in Transition

God caused the sea to roll back through a strong east wind and dried the seabed. With the water divided, the Hebrew people went across on dry ground. Once the last Hebrew stepped on the land on the other side, God closed the Red Sea, drowning Pharaoh's army.

God had promised them a land flowing with milk and honey, and the journey to Canaan should have taken around fourteen days. However, because of their disobedience and rebellion, they wandered in the wilderness for forty years. On one occasion, they considered Moses to be dead because he had been on the mountain with God for an extended period, so they decided to make a golden calf, which was an image of an Egyptian idol of worship. When Moses returned from the mountain, he heard singing coming from the camp, and upon his arrival, he saw the people were naked and participating in orgies (see Exodus 32:25), worshiping the golden calf. Paul wrote of their idolatry, fornication, and drunkenness (see 1 Corinthians 10:7–10).

God was not pleased with these lewd sinful acts, and all those over twenty-one years of age—the "older" generation—died in the wilderness. They had been miraculously delivered by God. They had been liberated—but in their minds, they were still in bondage. So, when they were confronted with difficulties, they reverted to what they were familiar with and desired to return to Egypt. Although delivered, the Hebrew people still had a slave mentality, a mentality of bondage. Mentally, they were tormented because they were torn between two lovers.

## Torn between Two Lovers

The Hebrew people found themselves in an uncomfortable position, one in which they were not willing to completely commit to either God or sin. They struggled with transitioning to a life of freedom and worship of the true God. They could not deny the miracle of God's parting the Red Sea and Him feeding them—the manna appeared from heaven every morning and quails every evening. However, in their minds, they were still accustomed to a life of bondage and humiliation. Once they were delivered, they could not have it both ways—they had to choose whom they would serve. Keep in mind that you, also, are a free moral agent, and God will never take away your free will or freedom of choice. The Lord Jesus said:

> No man can serve two masters: for either he will hate the one, and love the other, or else he will hold to the one, and despise the other. Ye cannot serve God and mammon.
>
> —Matthew 6:24

## A Life in Transition

When using the word *flesh*, we are speaking of more than the physical structure of man or the skin that overlies the skeleton. We are referring to the sin energy, or the sin force, that resides within the flesh. The sin force abides in the flesh of every person—the unsaved as well as those who are born again. The difference is that for unbelievers, the sin force is active and influencing their activities. On the other hand, for those who are saved, or born again, the sin force still resides in their flesh, but it has been rendered powerless because of what Jesus did for us on Calvary. Each person has "fallen in love with" sin from the time of their physical birth. Sinners are slaves of sin and Satan. Each of us has done its bidding.

Although we who are saved are no longer under the influence of sin, the sin force still resides within our fleshly bodies. This accounts for those inner evil urges or thoughts that believers experience at times. This knowledge is very important for spiritual "newborns" who may not understand why at times the old nature is pulling at them, why they feel so torn between two lovers. The will to please God and live a life of obedience will war inside of us with the desire to satisfy our fleshly needs. Remember, we cannot serve both. This struggle will continue for the entirety of our Christian lives—until the body dies. The apostle Paul wrote, "I find then a law, that, when I would do good, evil is present with me" (Romans 7:21). (You will learn the importance of mortifying the deeds of the body in chapter 9.)

A spiritual newborn needs to understand two things, especially during this important transition period. Having this knowledge will help him as he endeavors to walk in victory. First, the Bible states, "Who his own self [Jesus] bare our sins in his own body on the tree, that we, being dead to sins, should live unto righteousness: by whose stripes ye were healed" (1 Peter 2:24). I touched on this briefly in chapter 4: on the cross, in His body, Jesus bore the sins of all humanity—past, present, and future. However, because He did not eradicate our flesh, He knew those who would come to Him would still continue to struggle with the sin nature. However, by bearing our sins in His body, He obliterated the power sin had over believers and rendered it powerless in our lives. We are no longer obligated to serve sin. As a result of what Jesus secured for us on the cross, we should reckon ourselves dead, indeed, to sin and alive unto God through Jesus Christ (Romans 6:11). Listen, anything you don't feed will die, and when you don't give in to the lust and desires of your flesh, it will die also. (We will discuss this more in chapter 9, as well.)

The second thing a spiritual newborn needs to understand concerns the doctrine of circumcision. In Genesis

17, God implemented the covenant of circumcision with Abraham and his descendants, the Hebrew people. Abraham was instructed by God to circumcise the flesh of his foreskin to be a token of the covenant between God and himself and his people (see Genesis 17:11). Furthermore, God stated that every baby boy who was born in Abraham's house or brought into his household with money, or any stranger who became a part of his family, had to be circumcised to benefit from the covenant. This covenant of circumcision was a prelude, or type, of a spiritual circumcision that occurred at the point of salvation, when a person first came to Christ.

Paul, in his letter to the church of Colossae, wrote to the saints concerning spiritual circumcision:

> And ye are complete in him, which is
> the head of all principality and power: In
> whom also ye are circumcised with the circumcision made without hands, in putting
> off the body of the sins of the flesh by the
> circumcision of Christ: buried with him
> in baptism, wherein also ye are risen with
> him through the faith of the operation of
> God, who hath raised him from the dead.
>
> **—Colossians 2:10–13**

Paul wrote of Christians being circumcised with the circumcision made without hands. Simply put, this surgical procedure of cutting away the foreskin of the flesh (wherein lives the sin nature) from the inner man (representing the soul and spirit), is spiritually performed by the Holy Spirit. With this cutting away, or separation, of the flesh from the inner man, the sin energy no longer influences the activity of the inner man. Next, the Holy Spirit is fused together with the spirit of a believer. Paul uses the words "planted together" in Romans 6:5. To be "fused" or "planted together" illustrates a union, or oneness, with Christ Jesus. Thus, God the Holy Spirit now becomes the governing influence of the inner man. The effects of this union are seen through the physical life believers now live.

The visible activities of the body give a true reflection of who or what is influencing your inner man. God, in the Person of the indwelling Holy Spirit, has provided everything a newborn Christian would need to successfully overcome the sin nature and be transformed to live a Christlike life. Once loosed from sin's grip, the new convert has the freedom to worship and serve God in the beauty of holiness. Remember, earlier in this chapter I mentioned the concept of free will. God is not going to *make* us obey Him. We walk in obedience because we love Him. As we do so, we continue to mortify the flesh and grow in His love.

# CHAPTER 9

## *Mortifying the Deeds of the Body*

Throughout your Christian life, you will have to contend with the sin nature, which lives within the flesh. However, during the early stages of your Christian walk, you have the opportunity to develop a strong spiritual foundation, which will help you become victorious when you are tempted to sin. Remember, just as everything in the physical life is a learned behavior, so it also is in the spiritual life. You will learn to cling to Jesus because He is your strength. The Scripture tells us to "be strong in the Lord, and in the power of his might" (Ephesians 6:10). I do not mean to be repetitive, but our goal is to become Christlike in every area of our lives. This entails forsaking sin and abstaining from sinful practices. Many people are skeptical of those who teach that Christians can truly forsake sin; however, it is possible and *can* be achieved.

In Paul's letter to the church at Colossae, he introduces to those whom he is writing the word *mortify*, meaning "to put to death." Let's examine several passages of Scripture from the book of Colossians:

> So put to death and deprive of power the evil longings of your earthly body [with its sensual, self-centered instincts] immorality, impurity, sinful passion, evil desire, and greed, which is [a kind of] idolatry [because it replaces your devotion to God]. Because of these [sinful] things the [divine] wrath of God is coming on the sons of disobedience [those who fail to listen and who routinely and obstinately disregard God's precepts], and in these [sinful things] you also once walked, when you were habitually living in them [without the knowledge of Christ]. But now rid yourselves [completely] of all these things: anger, rage, malice, slander, and obscene (abusive, filthy, vulgar) language from your mouth. Do not lie to one another, for you have stripped off the old self with its evil practices.
>
> —**Colossians 3:5–9** AMP

There is a lot to unpack here, so let's begin with the fact that the sin nature, or the "flesh," has governed our lives from the day we were born into this world. The psalmist David said, "Behold, I was shapen in iniquity; and in sin did my mother conceive me" (Psalm 51:5). Prior to our salvation, we were addicted to sin. Every life action we took

## Mortifying the Deeds of the Body

was driven to satisfy the indulgences, cravings, and lusts of the flesh. We were totally under the influence of sin. Once we have been saved, we are not exempt from committing acts of sin or fulfilling the lusts of the flesh, even though we have been delivered from its power. We must take a firm stance against committing acts of sin because we love the Lord and we desire to please Him. Our Savior said, "Why call ye me, Lord, Lord, and do not the things which I say?" (Luke 6:46). We now understand that within the flesh, there dwells nothing good. So we as believers place no confidence in our flesh and its devices. Now, this also means we should try to avoid settings in which we are tempted to commit sin, even though the "body of sin" has been destroyed. We will discuss this more in detail under the heading "The Conflict Within."

Knowing that our old man is crucified (or put to death) with Christ, it is still the believer's responsibility to *keep* the sin nature dead by not submitting to it. Paul continued his discourse by adding, "Let not sin therefore reign in your mortal body, that ye should obey it in the lusts thereof. Neither yield ye your members as instruments of unrighteousness unto sin: But yield yourselves unto God, as those that are alive from the dead, and your members as instruments of righteousness unto God" (Romans 6:12–13).

In the text from Colossians above, the saints at Colossae were encouraged to "put to death" the sin nature and deprive it of its power. Anything you don't feed will eventually die. When you do not yield to sin or fleshly desires, you are depriving it of power; you are keeping it from having any influence over you.

Thus, we are encouraged to "neither give place to the devil" (Ephesians 4:27). God will never take away our freedom of choice. We must learn to trust Him, however, and willingly choose to do what is right when the opportunity to sin presents itself. Although we have lived in this "flesh suit"—our bodies—all our lives, now that we are saved, we are not obligated to serve it. We owe the flesh nothing! The Scripture declares, "Therefore, brethren, we are debtors, not to the flesh, to live after the flesh. For if ye live after the flesh, ye shall die: but if ye through the Spirit do mortify the deeds of the body ye shall live" (Romans 8:12–13).

This is a great time to take a moment to mention prayer and fasting. In our churches today, we often hear sermons about prayer, but we seldom speak about fasting. These two work together in our battle to mortify the flesh. We can define *prayer* as "personal communication with a holy, righteous, infinite God." Prayer is a two-way dia-

## Mortifying the Deeds of the Body

logue between ourselves and God. It is the only way we can communicate with God the Father. Prayer is such an integral part of our relationship with God that the Bible tells us to "pray without ceasing" (1 Thessalonians 5:17). People can be found praying throughout the Bible. Prayer is a time when we can commune with God and seek guidance and instructions about our lives. But prayer is so much more than making requests of the Lord; we also can confess our sins and seek His strength to overcome in any area of our lives where we are struggling. In fact, we would do better to talk with Him about it because He already knows our struggles!

When most people think of fasting, the only thought that comes to mind is abstaining from food. However, when we fast, what we are actually doing is denying the flesh what it is craving. That craving can equate to sinful, lustful desires. So we commit our fast to whatever we are attempting to overcome. Like we see people praying in the Scriptures, we also see people fasting throughout the Bible. The Scripture says, "Is not this the fast that I have chosen? to loose the bands of wickedness, to undo the heavy burdens, and to let the oppressed go free, and that ye break every yoke?" (Isaiah 58:6; see also Matthew 6:18). In the book of Ezra, we see prayer and fasting functioning together and yielding a positive response from God (Ezra 8:23).

Yes, salvation is God's free gift, but after the initial act of salvation, as we move forward on the journey of life, we must do our own part in mortifying the flesh, abstaining from sinful practices, and maintaining a life of purity. The Scriptures are very clear concerning this. The Bible says:

> Having therefore these promises, dearly beloved, let us cleanse ourselves from all filthiness of the flesh and spirit, perfecting holiness in the fear of God.
>
> **—2 Corinthians 7:1**

> And every man that hath this hope in him purifieth himself, even as he is pure.
>
> **—1 John 3:3**

In 2 Corinthians 7, the apostle Paul said we must cleanse ourselves. And in 1 John, the apostle John encouraged his readers by saying, "Every man that has this hope purifieth himself." The onus is on you, the believer, to do this. You may be asking yourself, *How does one cleanse or purify himself?* The answer is this: by remaining obedient and faithful to God and His Word. The only method of validating our love for God and His Son, Jesus, is through our obedience. Jesus said, "If you love Me, keep My commandments" (John 14:15 NKJV).

Paul continues his discourse in Colossians by instructing that unless you are married, all sexual sins, sinful passions, evil desire, greed, and idolatry must be put to death. Because of these sinful acts, God's wrath comes on those who disobey Him. Prior to being saved, we all sinned in these ways. Furthermore, Paul added, we should put off anger, rage, malice, slander, profanity, and vulgar language, and we are never to lie to one another. These make up the character of the old man, which we must put to death. Nonetheless, every Christian has engaged in this ongoing conflict between the flesh and the Spirit, which has fused Himself with your spirit, or inner man. Let's take a moment to address this.

## The Conflict Within

> This I say then, Walk in the Spirit, and ye shall not fulfill the lust of the flesh. For the flesh lusteth against the Spirit, and the Spirit against the flesh: and these are contrary the one to the other so that ye cannot do the things that ye would.
>
> **—Galatians 5:16–17**

As you continue in this Christian journey, over time you will realize that the biggest enemy you will ever confront is not the devil, but rather, your own flesh. The Scripture proclaims, "We have this treasure in earthen vessels" (2

Corinthians 4:7). We have the gift of salvation within a fleshly body that is corrupt. It is not the physical body that is saved, but it is the spiritual side of man (the soul and the spirit) that is saved. Even knowing the victory Jesus secured for us on Calvary, at times we still struggle and are confronted with the question, How do I consistently win the ongoing battle with my flesh? Every Christian should know how to control their body. Paul said, "Every one of you should know how to possess his vessel [body] in sanctification and honour" (1 Thessalonians 4:4). Keeping yourself in alignment with Christ and His will is paramount.

The Bible instructs us in times of temptation to "submit yourselves therefore to God. Resist the devil, and he will flee from you" (James 4:7). We must resist—and keep on resisting—the enemy and our fleshly desires. Although the enemy may leave for a season, he will return to tempt or entice you again. Remember, though, that anything you don't feed will eventually die. Each time you choose not to yield to fleshly passions, you are slowly mortifying them and starving them out of existence.

In Galatians 5, the apostle Paul reveals the key to becoming victorious in this conflict: we must be in constant subjection to the Holy Spirit. The Holy Spirit has taken up permanent residence within the believer, and He wants to live our lives for us, through us, but we must relinquish our control to Him. There is nothing we can achieve without the Holy Spirit's presence. So, Paul encouraged the saints at Galatia to "walk in the Spirit, and ye shall not fulfill the lust of the flesh" (Galatians 5:16). The word "walk" here refers to a way of living, how we act or conduct ourselves, how we order our manner of life or behavior. Daily, the believer must continually live in the Spirit, allowing Him to govern our affairs and strengthen us as He navigates us through this dark, evil world. If the Holy Spirit is ordering your steps, and you are walking in obedience to Him, you will not yield to the sinful desires of the flesh. I know the thought of not committing sin is challenging for many. However, we are to live a Spirit-led life. Just as God the Father and God the Son are holy and sinless, likewise is God the Holy Spirit. He would never tempt us or entice us to sin. The Scripture says, "God cannot be tempted with evil, neither tempteth he any man" (James 1:13).

In chapter 4, "The Holy Spirit and the Believer," I mentioned that the word *Comforter* another name for the "Holy Spirit." The word "comforter" is translated from the Greek word *parakletos*, which means "to come to one's aid," or "to come to one's side to assist." The Holy Spirit desires to assist us as we daily mortify the desires of the old nature.

However, we must be willing to allow Him to perform His perfect work within us.

*Lust* refers to strong desire, impulse, or passion of any kind, while *flesh* speaks of the totally depraved (sin) nature of the person who is void of God's presence. Therefore, the "lust of the flesh" refers to the evil desires, impulses, and passions constantly arising from within the sin nature of the unredeemed person. However, again, the influence the sin nature had over the unbeliever is broken when that person is saved, and a believer no longer has to obey it. However, it is still there, within the flesh, constantly attempting to rule over the believer as it did prior to their being saved.

The idea is for you to continually depend upon the Spirit to give you both the *desire* and the *power* to live a holy life, so that you will not bring to fulfillment the evil impulses of your fallen nature. You will be able to resist and overcome them! Again, Paul places upon the believer the responsibility of refusing to obey the sinful nature. This is the third time I have mentioned this in this chapter—that means it is important! We must come to grips with the fact that resisting the devil and mortifying the flesh is *our own* responsibility. The believer has been liberated from the enslavement to sin he experienced *before* salvation, and he

## Mortifying the Deeds of the Body

is *now* free to choose between right and wrong. As I have repeatedly said, God will never take away your freedom of choice.

The Holy Spirit was given to counteract this evil nature. When we willingly submit to His authority, He can aid us and keep us in the hour of temptation. Simply put, the Christian must cooperate with the Holy Spirit in His work of deliverance. Saying no to sin must mean no, while at the same time, we must trust the Holy Spirit to give us the power to overcome it. Therefore, the choice lies with us, as believers, as to whether we are going to submit to the instruction of the Holy Spirit or relent to the sin nature.

In Galatians 5:17, Paul continues to instruct the Church concerning the ongoing battle between the flesh and the Spirit. The Scripture teaches that these two are contrary, the one to the other, so that you cannot do the things that you would do. The word *contrary* means "to oppose or withstand." The flesh constantly has a strong desire to subdue the Spirit, and the Spirit constantly has a strong desire to subdue the flesh. These two are entrenched in an attitude of mutual opposition to one another. When the Holy Spirit places a course of conduct upon the heart of the believer, the flesh opposes the Spirit to prevent the believer from obeying those instructions. The purpose of each is to prevent the believer from doing what the other moves him to do.

The choice to yield to the flesh or walk in obedience lies with the believer. The Holy Spirit is not going to force you to live a life of obedience. I want to take a moment to reiterate this thought: You must be willing to absolutely surrender your will, to die to self and yield to the Spirit. That's your choice. Your victory and strength are in Him. Paul encouraged us to "be strong in the Lord, and in the power of his might" (Ephesians 6:10). In Galatians 5:19–23, Paul broke down the distinctive qualities and differences of each as he wrote, "Now the works of the flesh are manifest, which are these; adultery, fornication, uncleanness, lasciviousness, idolatry, witchcraft, hatred, variance, emulations, wrath, strife, seditions, heresies, envyings, murders, drunkenness, revellings, and such like: of the which I tell you before, as I have also told you in times past, that they which do such things shall not inherit the kingdom of God. But the fruit of the Spirit is love, joy, peace, longsuffering, gentleness, goodness, faith, meekness, temperance: against such there is no law."

The word *works* here refers to the deeds of the flesh, rather than the products of the evil nature. Prior to salvation, these deeds were a part of our everyday lives. It is these evil tendencies or sinful acts that are continually attempting to cause us to miss the mark and lapse back into a life of sin. The Spirit of God is attempting to suppress these attacks, while the flesh is constantly attempting to suppress the Spirit and His ability to keep us from falling. We must develop the habit of keeping our eyes fixed on the Lord Jesus and trust in the Holy Spirit. As we surrender and submit to the Holy Spirit, He can deposit His fruit and other virtues within our spirit. The fruit of the Holy Spirit is our new spiritual nature and can only be deposited within us by Him.

Previously in this chapter I alluded to Romans 7:18, which states, "For I know that in me (that is, in my flesh) dwelleth no good thing." In the transformation process, we must realize that there is nothing good about our old, fleshly nature; therefore, we should not have confidence in it (see Philippians 3:3). Paraphrasing the words of Paul found in Romans 7:18, the desire to live a godly life through the Holy Spirit is present, but to perform that which is good and right, we have not found a way to achieve it while trusting in the flesh. Paul shares with us his summation of the ongoing battle between flesh and the spirit man:

> I find then a law, that, when I would do
> good, evil is present with me. For I delight
> in the law of God after the inward man.

> But I see another law in my members, warring against the law of my mind, and bringing me into captivity to the law of sin which is in my members. O wretched man that I am! who shall deliver me from the body of this death? I thank God through Jesus Christ our Lord. So then with the mind I myself serve the law of God; but with the flesh the law of sin.
>
> **—Romans 7:21–25**

As Christians, every time we seek to do good, evil is present with us in the form of sin, which resides within the flesh. The inner man (our soul and our spirit) delights in the precepts of God, but there is another law operating within the flesh, which is warring against the precepts of God. This sensual dynamic operating within the flesh is determined to bring us back into spiritual bondage by luring us into sin, consequently causing separation from God and the God kind of life. Our warfare between the two is continual until we eventually take off this flesh suit through physical death. The summation is this: with the mind (the soul), we serve the law and precepts of God, but with the flesh, we are still tempted to serve the law of sin. As believers of Christ, we must continue in the ways of God and place no confidence in the flesh, that old, sinful nature. Therefore, our intellectual framework (our mind) must be renewed.

# CHAPTER 10

## *The Renewing of the Mind*

Within the mind, a war is constantly taking place. The mind is the battlefield where two spiritual entities battle for control, dominance, and supremacy. The battle of the mind is a hard-fought one. It is also a battle every single person faces, every single day. Your actions are influenced either by the flesh and demonic spirits (Ephesians 2:2–3) or by the Holy Spirit. The one in control over your thought process—your mind—is going to influence or dictate your life activities. Paul wrote, "We are destroying sophisticated arguments and every exalted and proud thing that sets itself up against the [true] knowledge of God, and we are taking every thought and purpose captive to the obedience of Christ" (2 Corinthians 10:5 AMP).

I think we can all agree it's much harder to take those thoughts captive and engage in the battle of the mind once those problematic thoughts gain momentum. We must learn to control our thoughts. Paul wrote in Philippians:

> Finally, brethren, whatsoever things are true, whatsoever things are honest, whatsoever things are just, whatsoever things

are pure, whatsoever things are lovely, whatsoever things are of good report: if there be any virtue, and if there be any praise, think on these things.

—**Philippians 4:8**

Every action and response of a person originates from within the mind. The mind or soul is the command center of the body. It houses the will, intellect, personality, feelings, desires, emotions, and appetite. When speaking of the "heart," the Bible in most cases is not speaking of the physical organ beating in a person's chest, but rather the deepest seat of a person's emotions and decisions, the soul. We see this in the translation of the Greek word for "heart," *kardia. Kardia* came to stand for the scope of man's entire mental and moral activity, both the rational and the emotional elements. It is the sphere of divine influence, the seat of a person's moral nature and spiritual life. Your thoughts represent who you are. You will eventually act out what you are contemplating or thinking.

In the Sermon on the Mount—Matthew 5 through 7—Jesus teaches us that our thoughts are judged first, as well as our actions, because every sinful deed originates from a thought within the mind. Jesus points out that a person's character is determined not so much by outward acts, but by the inward attitude that motivates the act. The outward act merely reflects the inward attitude of the heart. The Scripture says, "As [a man] thinketh in his heart, so is he" (Proverbs 23:7). Sin altered the mental framework of mankind, changing it from its original created state. Thus, a renewing of the spiritual mind must take place. Again, let's refer back to Genesis to gain a better understanding of the intellectual framework of fallen man.

> And God saw that the wickedness of man was great in the earth, and that every imagination of the thoughts of his heart was only evil continually.
>
> **—Genesis 6:5**

Due to the importance of this passage of Scripture as it reflects the mindset of fallen man, I want to focus on some of the key words within this verse. The first is *wickedness*. In a Hebrew word study of *wickedness*, we find in the definition terms such as *vicious in disposition*, *unpleasant*, *misery*, and *distress*. This thought process of man was completely opposite from the man whom God created after His own likeness and image, Adam. Moreover, man had not been long removed from Eden, and he was already in this mental condition; this should warn us about giving place to the devil. Paul said that "a little leaven leaveneth the whole lump" (Galatians 5:9). Simply put, unrepented sins will permeate your whole spiritual being.

Second, the word *imagination* in Hebrew speaks of the intellectual framework of man; basically, it corresponds with the word *thoughts*. Defining the word *thoughts* from the Hebrew references words such as *devices*, *plans*, and *purpose*. *Heart*, as defined by the Hebrew word *leb*, speaks of the inner man and uses terms such as *soul*, *mind*, *understanding*, *knowledge*, *thinking*, *emotions*, and *memory*. The word *evil*, in Hebrew, speaks of being *bad*, *evil*, *malignant*, *unpleasant*, and *disagreeable*. The thought process of mankind is in a state of constant rebellion against God. Due to the wickedness of man, God caused it to rain upon the earth—a great flood. This flood purged all life from the face of the earth, except for Noah, his family, and the animals within the ark; however, it did not change the mental framework of fallen mankind. After the water abated from the earth, God said, "I will not again curse the ground any more for man's sake; for the imagination of man's heart is evil from his youth" (Genesis 8:21). This rebellious mindset is still within every person who enters this life today. When a person is born again, their mind must be renewed. Change begins with your thought process. A person cannot succeed as a Christian with a carnal, or worldly, mind.

## Spiritual Mind Renewal

Just as everything in the physical realm is a learned behavior, likewise, so is everything in the spiritual realm. Under the tutelage of the Holy Spirit and the Word of God, the walls of our old intellectual framework are demolished, and a renovation of our thought processes takes place, causing us to think as Christ thought. According to Hebrews 9:14, the moment you were saved, the blood of Christ purged your conscience from dead works to serve the living God. To *purge* means "to cleanse." Jesus the Messiah, through the eternal Spirit, offered Himself without spot or blemish to God. What made the blood of Jesus so unique was that He, in His Person, was spotless—absolutely holy and perfectly righteous. Thus, His blood could satisfy God's righteous demand and could cleanse, or purge, men's conscience from sin and dead works. The word *conscience* means the faculty by which we understand the will of God, as that which is designed to govern our lives.

The sacrifice of Jesus reaches the very center of the moral and spiritual being of the individual. It cleanses the conscience of dead works, in that it changes the character of the works of the individual. Before salvation, the sinner did so-called good works in the strength of his own sinful nature. However, they were dead works, lifeless works, because they were not in alignment with God's will. After salvation, a radical transformation within the individual occurred, producing good works through the power and presence of the Holy Spirit living within them.

With the conscience, or mental framework, now cleansed, the Holy Spirit has a clean canvas to work with, and the renewing process can begin. The Holy Spirit is the only One who has the power to renew the mind as we die to self and obey His instructions. I want to refer you to two passages of Scripture:

> That ye put off concerning the former conversation the old man, which is corrupt according to the deceitful lusts: and be renewed in the spirit of your mind; and that ye put on the new man, which after God is created in righteousness and true holiness.
>
> **—Ephesians 4:22–24**

> And be not conformed to this world: but be ye transformed by the renewing of the mind, that ye may prove what is that good, and acceptable, and perfect, will of God.
>
> **—Romans 12:2**

In the text from Ephesians, we see the word *conversa-*

*tion*. This word is not speaking of an act of communication with someone; rather, it's referring to behavior, the way a person acts. Paul instructs us to put off or, put away, our former behavior, which reflected the nature of the old man. In chapter 8, "Mortifying the Deeds of the Body," I referred to Galatians 5:19–21, various sins are listed, known as the works of the flesh or the garments in which the old man was clothed—which are useless to the believer in Christ.

These useless garments should no longer be a part of the fabric of our new life in Christ. Clinging to them will affect your relationship with the Lord in a negative manner. We are to discard the works of the flesh because they are corrupt, according to deceitful lust. This corrupt nature is a progressive condition; the more one dabbles in sin, the worse one will become. We know that lust is a strong craving or a passionate desire, whether good or evil. Here it refers to evil cravings. Within the Church today, we see the spirit of wantonness, the lust for material things, and wealth operating in many and destroying their relationship with God. As a believer, especially if you are a new convert, you cannot allow yourself to become caught up or ensnared by lustful and worldly desires.

Many Christians struggle due to a lack of knowledge of the life they have been saved to live. Therefore, they continue to allow fleshly impulses to govern their lives. Therefore, it so important that new converts receive sound foundational, biblical teaching. Knowledge of the truth and the life one has been saved to live is so very important. As you begin this new journey in Christ, remember that salvation takes place the moment you confess and repent of your sins; however, sanctification is a lifelong process. We don't become Christlike overnight. So, don't become "weary in well doing: for in due season we shall reap, if we faint not" (Galatians 6:9).

Ridding ourselves of our old behavior patterns begins with the renewing of the mind. When we think of something being "renovated" or "renewed," we think of it being restored to its original state or condition. The renewing of your mental faculties is accomplished by God the Holy Spirit in the inward man. This renewing is transitional and continuing; it is part of the sanctification process. Throughout our Christian lives, the Holy Spirit will be renewing the spirit of our mind.

The word *spirit* refers to the individual's human spirit—the part of man that gives him a God-consciousness. It is the higher life principle in man. The renewal takes place, not in the mind itself, but in the spirit of it. This change, or renewal, radically alters the entire sphere of the inner mechanism as God the Holy Spirit imparts His nature and virtue within the believer.

Next, Paul instructs us to put on the new man. The "new man" refers to the person who has been born again and is now influenced by the divine nature. This new man is created after God, or after the pattern of what God is. In chapter 1, I briefly referenced a passage of Scripture in Ephesians, which states, "For we are his workmanship, created in Christ Jesus unto good works which God hath before ordained that we should walk in them" (Ephesians 2:10). The Greek word for "created" used here is *kitzo*, which is the Greek equivalent to the Hebrew word *bara*, found in Genesis 1:26–27. Only God can create or bring forth something from nothing. Man was created spiritually in the likeness and image of God. When a person becomes born again, the inner man, which was dead because of sin, is now quickened and made spiritually alive in Christ. It is restored back to its original spiritual state, having received eternal life. We are God's spiritual handiwork, created by Him and made a new spiritual creature through Him.

This new man, who is created after God's likeness, is created in righteousness and true holiness, created after the pattern of what God is. God is holy, so when you are in union with Christ, you are holy also. Our holiness comes from His holiness, as it is written: "But as he which hath called you is holy, so be ye holy in all manner of conversation. Because it is written, Be ye holy; for I am holy" (1 Peter 1:15–16). The word *holy* here speaks of the idea of purity, freedom from sin. The believer is holy, both in the sense of being set apart for His use, and in the sense of being used for pure and righteous purposes. Thus, the believer is free from sinful practices. I don't want to seem repetitious, but God has called us to a life of separation from sin. Simply put, as a believer in Christ Jesus, we should not indulge in the sinful practices of the flesh and the world. This cannot be stressed enough. Keep in mind: "the soul that sinneth, it shall die" (Ezekiel 18:4). Righteousness indicates a positional change. Every person who has benefited from the grace of God and believed on the Lord Jesus for salvation is brought into right relationship with Him.

In Romans 12:2, Paul urges us not to conform to this world system. The word *conformed* means "to fashion or shape one thing like another." As we are no longer under the influence of the sin nature and the power of darkness, we as Christians should not continue to live as if we are not saved. Simply put, we must stop assuming an outward lifestyle that is patterned after this world, a lifestyle that does not reflect who you are in your inner being as a born-again child of God. In many instances today, it's hard to distinguish Christians from those who are still unregenerated and living worldly lives. We talk, dress, and act as if we have not experienced Jesus Christ and His saving grace. In some ways, many churches have incorporated worldly methods and tactics to fill the pews. Gimmicks and gadgets are not going to bring us into a right relationship with God. God has given us the best bait with which to fish: His Word; however, some messages I have heard coming from the pulpit today are so diluted they could not persuade anyone to come to Christ Jesus. Christians can walk around in denial, but remember, it was Jesus who said the condition of the end-times churches made Him sick. He said, "So then because thou art lukewarm, and neither cold nor hot, I will spue thee out of my mouth" (Revelation 3:16). The word *spue* here means "to vomit," indicating something so nauseating that it had to be vomited up.

Those who have experienced a God-encounter and been born again should not continue to live lives that are not a reflection of the inner change they have experienced. Being now children of the light, there is no need to live a life of conformity to this world system of darkness. The mannerisms, speech, expressions, styles, and habits of the believer in Christ must change. Transformation must occur, and this is accomplished by the renewing of the mind or the thought process. Remember, the process of the Holy

Spirit renewing your mind will continue throughout your Christian life.

The word *renewing* in Romans 12:2 speaks of a gradual conforming of the man, more and more, to that new spiritual world into which he has been introduced, and in which he now lives. The aim of the Holy Spirit in this renewing work is to put sin out of the believer's life and produce His own fruit as the believer surrenders and dedicates his life to Christ. God the Holy Spirit wants to saturate your soul with the Word and engraft it within your mind. As you consecrate yourself to God all the more, He can reveal Himself to you more and more. The key to maximizing your life and relationship with Christ is knowledge and obedience to God's Word. We must trust and depend on the Holy Spirit to reveal His truth so that we can successfully live the life that God requires of us.

# CHAPTER 11

## *Growth through Knowledge*

The *Webster's New College Dictionary* defines *knowledge* as "the act, fact, or state of knowing." The dictionary also defines *learning* "as obtaining knowledge of a subject, skill, art, by studying, experience, and instruction." In the second installment of the *Star Wars* series, Luke Skywalker sought out Yoda, a Jedi master, to begin his training as a Jedi Knight and obtain knowledge of the Force. The first lesson was learning the power of the Force and how to effectively use it. Learning the Force was essential in becoming a Jedi, so Master Yoda put Luke through various tests that would test his ability to use the Force. After failing several times to remove his space fighter from the swamp, Luke became frustrated and said, "You are asking me to do the impossible."

So, Yoda demonstrated the power of the Force by focusing on Luke's space fighter, which was buried in the swamp, and levitating it over to dry land. Watching this in amazement, Luke asked why he couldn't do that himself. Yoda shared with Luke two character flaws that were hindering his growth as a Jedi, preventing him from successfully using the power of the Force. The first was that he had to *unlearn* all that he had learned and *learn a new way*. Second, Yoda said, Luke couldn't remove his fighter from the swamp because of his *unbelief*; simply put, his lack of faith was preventing him from doing what he was meant to do.

Those two statements can be applied to every person who has been born again. First, we must unlearn all the sinful practices our old nature taught us from birth and allow the Holy Spirit to reveal a new and better way of living. It is written in 1 Corinthians:

> Eye hath not seen, nor ear heard, neither have entered into the heart of man, the things which God hath prepared for them that love Him. But God hath revealed them unto us by his Spirit: for the Spirit searcheth all things, yea, the deep things of God.
>
> —1 Corinthians 2:9–10

A new life requires a new perspective that can only be provided through a new spiritual teacher. That Teacher is the Holy Spirit. As you seek His guidance and study the Scriptures, He will teach you and give you revelations of truth. Some things in life cannot be comprehended by human intelligence and logic alone. The deeper revelations of truth are only revealed by the Holy Spirit, to those who seek a deeper understanding of God's Word. He will also engraft the Word within your heart (soul). The learning process will be challenging and arduous, due to the ongoing battle with the sin nature. Believers are implored to rid themselves of the old way of thinking, which is a hindrance to your faith to believe and receive His promises.

A spiritual transformation of the thought process must occur. In essence, we are what we think, and our thoughts are based on the knowledge we have. The book of Proverbs declares, "For as he thinketh in his heart, so is he" (Proverbs 23:7).

Second, unbelief will prevent you from maximizing your experience in Christ. The truth of the matter is that unbelief is a sin. Romans 14:23 declares, "For whatsoever is not of faith is sin." Do you truly believe you can achieve all that God has commissioned you to do? While Jesus was on the earth, He called twelve men together and gave them power and authority over all devils, to heal the sick, and to preach the kingdom of God (Luke 9:1).

On a certain day, Jesus took Peter, James, and John to a high mountain and was transfigured before them (Matthew 17:1–5). The remaining nine disciples who were left at the camp were totally unaware of the impending test that would try their faith. When the Transfiguration was complete and they came down off the mountain, they encountered a father who brought his son who was possessed with a devil to the nine, but they could not cast the devil out of the young man (Matthew 17:14–20). Nine men who had been empowered by Jesus to deal with these very matters could not carry out what they had been commissioned to do. Upon Jesus' return from the mountain and seeing the commotion, the boy's father explained to Him what had taken place, and then Jesus cast the demon out of the young boy. Afterward, the nine disciples came to Jesus asking why they could not cast the demon out. Jesus responded, "Because of your unbelief" (Matthew 17:20). Knowing what we are empowered to do and having faith to do it are two separate things. We will further discuss this in greater detail in this chapter under the heading "Practical Application."

Knowledge of the Christian life is a necessary item in our spiritual toolbox. A person cannot effectively live a life without knowledge and understanding of what that life demands. The Scripture proclaims, "My people are destroyed for lack of knowledge" (Hosea 4:6). We are living in a season when men will not endure sound teaching. People do not like to be told how they should live their lives, not from God, not from the holy Scriptures, and not from anyone else. God's plan for humanity is rejected because men are not willing to conform to the truth and live a life of obedience to Him. Jesus declared,

> Light is come into the world, and men loved darkness rather than light, because their deeds were evil. For every one that doeth evil hateth the light, neither cometh to the light, lest his deeds should be reproved.
>
> **—John 3:19–20**

The Christian life is a spiritual life that is lived through the power of the Holy Spirit and is totally opposite of the fleshly, sinful life from which you were delivered. As I wrote earlier in this book, we can't love both; we cannot be servants of two masters. In chapter 8, I wrote that every life experience is the result of learned behavior. Born of the flesh, we have all learned the ways of the sin nature that resides in our flesh; in fact, it governed our lives. In some instances, we may carry over a particular sin into the new life. However, as it is written, we must lay aside every weight, every hindrance, and any sin that impedes the growth process. As believers, we should willingly lay aside that which impedes our spiritual growth, rather than asking God to take it away. Now that a born-again experience has taken place, we must learn what God requires of us. Consider the words of Colossians 3:9–10. We are told to take off the "old man" with his sinful deeds and be clothed in the "new man," which is renewed in knowledge; this knowledge comes from God, who created us. Again, we are encouraged to take it off from us, as if we are taking off a garment we no longer need, which are the sinful habits of the old man. Afterward, we are to clothe ourselves with the garments of the new man, who is renewed in the perfect knowledge of Christ. Prior to Adam's fall, he had complete and perfect knowledge. Adam was created having Godlike intellectual capabilities. Simply put, he thought as God thought. Christians today should think as Jesus thought. The Scriptures clearly states, "We have the mind of Christ" (1 Corinthians 2:16). Every believer should begin to develop Godlike intelligence as they yield themselves to the Holy Spirit.

Why is knowledge so important? We can't effectively live the Christian life without knowing what God requires. The believer should not continue in a carnal state on the same old life journey. We see the struggles of the saints at Corinth and Paul saying to them, "For ye are yet carnal: for whereas there is among you envying, and strife, and divisions, are ye not carnal, and walk as men" (1 Corinthians 3:3). The word *carnal* speaks of the sinful element of men's fleshly human nature. A person who is considered

## Growth through Knowledge

carnal is still governed by the sin nature and will continue to practice sin. Peter exhorts believers to "abstain from fleshly lusts, which war against the soul" (1 Peter 2:11).

Again, I often say that the biggest battle you will fight as a believer is against yourself, meaning your fleshly nature. How do we control it or respond when the old nature attempts to seize dominance over us? In 1 Peter 2:11, the Bible describes believers as "pilgrims" and "strangers temporarily living in a foreign land." The world of darkness is no longer our home; neither are we governed by the passions of this world. Therefore, we ought to refrain from sinful desires or passions because they war against the soul.

This warfare will be ongoing throughout our lifetime. The human will is wicked, and yielding to sinful desires will affect your experience and relationship with God. No matter what people may say, or how they feel, the person who continually participates in sinful behavior will die, for the price for sinning is death. That fact will never change. We must overcome sinful practices; remember, people are destroyed because of their lack of knowledge. We must continue to grow in our knowledge of God's Word.

Knowledge of God's Word develops Christlikeness or Christlike characteristics. Knowledge also produces faith—faith to believe, trust, and stand on God promises. The Scriptures are the road map that will navigate us through this dark, evil, godless world. David said, "Thy word is a lamp unto my feet, and a light unto my path" (Psalm 119:105). As we apply the Scriptures to our lives on a daily basis, they will illuminate the dark areas, giving us the opportunity to repent. God's Word will find you. It's alive and powerful, and it can reach places within you that are unreachable by even the best surgeons. It can discern every thought and knows all your intentions. Thus, every time we meditate on, study, or read the Scriptures, they are cleansing us and setting us apart to be use of God.

In the armament of the Christian solider, the only offensive weapon is described as the "sword of the Spirit, which is the word of God" (Ephesians 6:17). We cannot become skillful swordsmen without the knowledge of God's Word and how to apply it. To experience a wholesome, meaningful relationship, we must take time to get to know the other person. In our relationship with God, He knows all about us, and now we must learn of Him and what necessitates being Christlike and a Kingdom citizen.

## Learning to Live from Christ's Example

Paul instructed the saints at Corinth to "be ye followers

## Growth through Knowledge

of me, even as I also am of Christ" (1 Corinthians 11:1). The only true example or pattern of the Christian life we have to follow is the life Jesus lived. In fact, Jesus told His followers to learn of Him (Matthew 11:29). He set the precedent we should follow. In his letter to the church at Philippi, Paul expressed his desire to learn and experience the life of Jesus. He wrote, "That I may know him, and the power of his resurrection, and the fellowship of his sufferings, being made conformable unto his death" (Philippians 3:10). This verse encapsulates, or gives a complete summation of, how intimate Paul's relationship was with Jesus—and how ours should be. Every believer should strongly desire to experience all our Savior experienced, learning from Christ, who provided an illustration of the life we should live—sufferings and all.

Paul begins this passage by expressing his desire to "know him." The word *know* here speaks of familiarity and intimacy. The Church, being the bride of Christ, should have an intimate relationship with Jesus, the Bridegroom, experiencing all He has made available to His bride. We should desire to become thoroughly acquainted with Him. Your eternal resting place is at stake here, and we truly need to know and understand what pleases our Savior and flee from what doesn't. We must grow to appreciate His great love and mercy. We were helpless to change the condition in which we existed in this life—as sinners. Yet Jesus loved us in spite of our sinful, rebellious nature; He took our place on the cross so that we could be reconciled to Him. Paul wanted to have a complete understanding and knowledge of Jesus. As we learn and gain a more complete understanding of who Jesus is and His personality, we can began to understand how Christ lived and the need to imitate, or mimic, His life. The apostle John wrote, "He that saith he abideth in him ought himself also so to walk [live], even as he walked [lived]" (1 John 2:6).

Paul continued by saying he wanted to experience the power of Jesus' resurrection. The resurrected life is a life of supernatural spiritual change, deliverance, and victory over sin, flesh, and the devil. This life is active in every believer. Sadly, many never truly experience the resurrected life, because they tend to cleave to the old life and never die to their flesh. Thus, they are carnal, and to be carnally minded is death. The Bible proclaims that if we have partaken of the resurrection of Jesus, we should walk in newness of life (Romans 6:4–6).

Paul continued his discourse by stating he wanted to share in the fellowship of His sufferings. I truly believe that Christians today do not understand what Christian suffering actually is. When the Scriptures speak of suffering, it's referring to suffering for Christ, for righteousness, for standing for the Gospel, for not compromising godly principles. Jesus, Paul, Peter, James, and many of the apostles and Christians of the Church were martyred because of their testimonies. Christian suffering does not mean you are struggling financially because you have overspent your budget and now you are in debt. Christian suffering is not becoming ill within your body because you have abused it with cigarettes, liquor, or drugs. I would like to encourage you to read the eleventh chapter of Hebrews, what many call the "roll call" of the heroes of faith. While you are reading, give careful attention to Hebrews 11:32–40, as the writer details the suffering of the saints. Paul said, "All that will live godly in Christ Jesus shall suffer persecution" (2 Timothy 3:12). Are you willing to experience persecution for the sake of Jesus and the Gospel?

In the book of Romans, Paul connects us with being heirs and our inheritance to suffering. The Scriptures states, "The Spirit itself beareth witness with our spirit, that we are the children of God: and if children, then heirs; heirs of God, and joint heirs with Christ; if so be that we suffer with him, that we may be also glorified together. For I reckon that the suffering of this present time are not worthy to be compared with the glory which shall be revealed in us" (Romans 8:16–18). Everyone wants to be an heir and partake of God's promises and blessings; however, not everyone is willing to partake of the sufferings that Jesus and many of the apostles experienced. As Christians, suffering and persecution becomes a badge of honor that we should wear with great joy.

The Scriptures, speaking of one of the accounts of Paul's suffering, says, "And there came thither certain Jews from Antioch and Iconium, who persuaded the people, and having stoned Paul, drew him out of the city, supposing he had been dead. Howbeit, as the disciples stood round about him, he rose up, and came into the city: and the next day he departed with Barnabas to Derbe. And when they had preached the gospel to that city, and had taught many, they returned again to Lystra, and to Iconium, and Antioch, confirming the souls of the disciples, and exhorting them to continue in the faith, and that we must through much tribulation enter into the kingdom of God" (Acts 14:19–22). Looking back at the text from Philippians, Paul concluded by saying that inwardly, he wanted to be conformed into Jesus' likeness, even to His death, dying as He did. In Acts 14:19–22, we read that Paul was stoned, even to the point of death, for the defense of the Gospel. The Scripture says that Jesus told His disciples they would be "witnesses unto me" (Acts 1:8). The word *witnesses* is a translation of the Greek word *martus*, which speaks of those who, after

His example, have proven the strength and genuineness of their faith in Christ by undergoing a violent death.

We know that later in his life, Paul truly died a martyr's death, for the testimony of Jesus. In 2 Corinthians, the apostle Paul shared with us a summary of his sufferings:

> Are they ministers of Christ? (I speak as a fool) I am more; in labours more abundant, in stripes above measure, in prisons more frequent, in deaths oft. Of the Jews five times received I forty stripes save one. Thrice was I beaten with rods, once was I stoned, thrice I suffered shipwreck, a night and a day I have been in the deep; in journeyings often, in perils of waters, in perils of robbers, in perils by mine own countrymen, in perils by the heathen, in perils in the city, in perils in the wilderness, in perils in the sea, in perils among false brethren; in weariness and painfulness, in watchings often, in hunger and thirst, in fastings often, in cold and nakedness.
>
> **—2 Corinthians 11:23–27**

Looking at the definition of the word *tribulation*, one word sticks out: *affliction*. David wrote, "Many are the afflictions of the righteous: but the Lord delivereth him out of them all (Psalm 34:19). True believers have learned to take up their cross and continue to follow Jesus Christ, applying the principles of the Word to their lives daily.

## Practical Application

When I speak of practical application, I am speaking of applying or putting into practice that which has been taught, learned, or revealed. Knowledge is powerful; however, if it is never applied, it is useless and therefore unproductive. In simple terms, an application is the response and action that follows our hearing God's Word. Applying the Scriptures is the duty of all Christians. If not applied, the Bible becomes nothing more to us than a normal book, an impractical collection of old manuscripts. Paul says, "Whatever you have learned or received or heard from me, or seen in me—put it into practice. And the God of peace will be with you" (Philippians 4:9 NIV). When we do apply the Bible, however, God Himself will be with us.

The Bible is God's way of revealing Himself to us. When we apply the Scriptures to our lives, we move from simply having *head knowledge* toward also having *heart knowledge* of God's Word. The Word must become a living *rhema* within the heart (the soul). As we delve deeper into our application of God's Word, we can view it from two parts—our internal response and our external actions.

## Growth through Knowledge

Our internal response is the heartfelt desire and intellectual decision to act on God's Word. Our external action is the fulfillment of that desire and decision. Both sides of this equation must be operational in order to have effective application.

One side alone of the response-and-action equation is not acceptable for true application. Without a genuine internal response, our external actions may be misguided, and without authentic external actions, our internal responses may prove ineffective. Anyone can read the Bible and think they know God, but only those to whom the Spirit has revealed the truth of the Scriptures will truly come to know Him. In James 1:22, the Scriptures confirm that hearing is not enough; there must be application of that which has been heard. It states, "But be ye doers of the word, and not hearers only, deceiving your own selves." We must apply God's Word to our lives.

In the process of sanctification and relationship-building, God uses His Word to reveal Himself to us. He also uses His Word to reveal what we need to do to become the bride for whom He's returning, as well as what we may need to work on or walk away from. We listen to sermons, we read the Scriptures, but are we daily applying what the Spirit has revealed to our lives? Are we trusting in God's

Word, or are we still depending on our own human will? Remember, the human will is wicked and opposes everything the Scriptures are revealing as they point out our character flaws. Jesus said, "Ye are clean through the word which I have spoken unto you" (John 15:3). Are we willing to allow the Word to cleanse us? To sanctify us?

Several things within the mental framework of man must occur before we arrive at the point where we can apply the Scriptures to our lives. It begins with our spirit—the soil in which the Word is being sown—simply, the state of our soul, our intellectual framework. Let's examine both.

We must have a teachable spirit and heart. The Scripture says, "My people are destroyed for lack of knowledge: because thou hast rejected knowledge, I will also reject thee" (Hosea 4:6). We can't apply God's principles to our lives if we do not know them. People perish because of their lack of knowledge of the Scriptures. Furthermore, people will often reject knowledge because they really don't want to know or hear the truth, but if you reject true knowledge, God has said He will reject you.

We must consider the condition of the soil of our soul. Is the soil of our hearts (souls), conducive to receiving the truth? Has the soil been tilled, so that anything that may prevent the seed of the Word from growing has been removed or uprooted? In the parable of the sower, found in Mark 4:14–20, Jesus taught on the various levels of receptivity of those who hear the Word. Jesus said, "The sower soweth the word" (verse 14). Every time you hear God's Word it is like a farmer is sowing seed into the ground—and we know that every seed that is planted does not germinate and produce life.

Let's look at the four conditions of the heart Jesus taught about, and see what category you fall into. Everyone will fit into one of these groups.

*The indifferent hearers, those on the wayside*: These people are still carnal, and their hearts are hardened and reject the truth because they are not willing to conform to it. When they hear the Word, Satan immediately takes away the Word that was sown in their hearts; thus, the Word sown cannot produce life.

*The emotional hearers.* These are those who receive the Word with gladness. You may know someone like that. They become excited when they hear the Word—but they never change, and they never conform to it. You can call them an hour after a worship service has ended, and they can't even tell you what the message was about. The problem is that they are not grounded, not deeply rooted in the Lord, and they have too many other things going on in their lives—things that should not be taking place. Thus, when they are persecuted because of the way they are living, or when the Word convicts them, they become offended. These hearers will only endure for a time.

*The worldly hearers.* These are those who hear the Word but who have other things in their lives that they prioritize over the Word. These include worldly cares, the deceitfulness of riches, and evil desires, the lust of other things. These things hinder the ability of the seed of God's Word to take root; thus, no fruit is produced. Greed, the spirit of wantonness, worldly ambitions, and lustful desires must cease in our lives.

*The receptive hearers.* These are the ones Jesus describes as "good ground." These are the ones whose hearts are receptive to the Word. They hear the Word, they receive it, and they apply it to their lives. The seed of the Word germinates and produces fruit within the believer with an increase of some thirtyfold, some sixtyfold, and some hundredfold. It is God's desire that we bring forth much fruit. Having more fruit means that you will resemble Christ more, applying His principles to your life daily.

Align your life with what the Bible says. The Scripture says, "All scripture is given by inspiration of God, and is profitable for doctrine, for reproof, for correction, for instruction in righteousness: That the man of God may be perfect, thoroughly furnished unto all good works" (2 Timothy 3:16–17). Apply the Scriptures by aligning your life with what it says. Sometimes we read the Bible and notice that it contradicts our lifestyle; it is exposing active sin in our lives. At that point, something must change. The Bible is infallible; therefore, it is we who need to change; it is we who need to conform and align our lives to the Scriptures. Everyone at some point will need correction. This is often the most difficult area of application. Correction involves taking the necessary steps to align our attitudes and actions with God and His Word. Remember, the Holy Spirit helps us with this. When the Scriptures convict us of sin or other shortcomings, the Holy Spirit helps to deliver us and transform us—as we submit to Him. I want to conclude with these words of Jesus: "Therefore whosoever heareth these sayings of mine, and doeth them, I will liken him unto a wise man, which built his house upon a rock: And the rain descended, and the floods came, and the winds blew, and beat upon that house; and it fell not: for it was founded upon a rock. And everyone that heareth these sayings of mine, and doeth them not, shall be likened unto a foolish man, which built his house upon the sand: And the rain descended, and the floods came, and the winds blew, and beat upon that house; and it fell; and great was the fall of it" (Matthew 7:24–27).

## Good Application Comes from Good Interpretation

> Knowing this first, that no prophecy of the scripture is of any private interpretation.
>
> —2 Peter 1:20

Can we truly apply the Scriptures to our lives without a true interpretation of the Scriptures and the subsequent life we are instructed to live? Application of the Word of God is paramount for the believer in Christ. There is no victory, no faith, no Christlikeness, without the Word of God being alive and active in our lives. Therefore, it is absolutely necessary to have an accurate interpretation of the Scriptures. If we interpret them incorrectly, we will most likely end up applying them incorrectly, too. This is dangerous because it can potentially lead us to build our lives on a lie instead of the truth. Peter states that there should be no private interpretation of Scripture. If we are led by the Holy Spirit, we will come to the same understanding of the Scriptures as other believers, although different people may articulate these truths differently. When speaking with someone about a passage of Scripture, if they say, "In my mind I came to this conclusion . . ." or "This is how I see that passage of Scripture . . ." red flags should immediately go up. Many people are attempting to understand and reason with the Scriptures through their sense knowledge.

## Growth through Knowledge

But understanding Scripture does not come down to your opinion or point of view. This is why the spirit of error is so prevalent in the body of Christ today.

We must rely on the Holy Spirit to give us the correct interpretation of Scripture. This is called *revelation*. Let's look at a passage of Scripture found in 1 Corinthians.

> For God has unveiled them and revealed them to us through the [Holy] Spirit; for the Spirit searches all things [diligently], even [sounding and measuring] the [profound] depths of God [the divine counsels and things far beyond human understanding]. For what person knows the thoughts and motives of a man except the man's spirit within him? So also no one knows the thoughts of God except the Spirit of God. Now we have received, not the spirit of the world, but the [Holy] Spirit who is from God. . . . We also speak of these things, not in words taught or supplied by human wisdom, but in those taught by the Spirit, combining and interpreting spiritual thoughts with spiritual words [for those being guided by the Holy Spirit.
>
> **—1 Corinthians 2:10–13** AMP

Often, when people want interpretation or understanding of a passage of Scripture, they consult their pastor or someone they know who is in ministry, someone who is grounded in the faith. However, on numerous occasions, we fail to consult God Himself for guidance, instruction, and interpretation from the Holy Spirit. The Bible is a spiritual book, and so true revelation and interpretation can only be obtained from the Holy Spirit. God the Father has promised to give the Holy Spirit to every believer, and He, the Spirit, would teach us and reveal biblical truth that is far beyond human comprehension. Jesus said, "But the Comforter, which is the Holy Ghost, whom the Father will send in my name, he shall teach you all things, and bring all things to your remembrance" (John 14:26).

The Scriptures bear witness to the Holy Spirit as our spiritual Teacher, sent from God. The passage states, "But the anointing which ye have received of him abideth in you, and ye need not that any man teach you: but as the same anointing teacheth you of all things, and is truth, and is no lie, and even as it hath taught you, ye shall abide in him" (1 John 2:27). The interpretation and revelations we receive from the Holy Spirit are true and not erroneous. In the Corinthians text, Paul said the Holy Spirit would reveal to us things we can't begin to comprehend with the human senses—even the deeper mysteries of God. To *re-*

*veal* means "to uncover, to unveil." Simply put, the Holy Spirit reveals to believers that which was once covered or hidden. No man knows the things of God, but the Spirit of God communicates to every Christian His plan for their lives. Now it's up to us to apply that which has been revealed and walk in obedience to it. God loves us deeply, and He has plans for each one of us. These plans include using us as His vessels to share the Gospel message of Jesus Christ. As we apply Scripture to our lives with the Holy Spirit's guidance, transformation will begin to take place. We must give the Holy Spirit something to work with; that's why we continue to study God's Word and seek Him daily.

## Reading the Scriptures versus Studying the Scriptures

> Study to shew thyself approved unto God, a workman that needeth not to be ashamed, rightly dividing the word of truth.
>
> **—2 Timothy 2:15**

While studying certainly involves reading, reading is not the same as studying. To *study* God's Word means that we must prayerfully devote time and attention to acquiring advance knowledge on a particular subject, person, or book of the Bible. Many people read the Bible daily and spend a lifetime *on the surface* of the Word of God. However, as Paul stated in 1 Corinthians 2:10, there are many deeper things the Holy Spirit wants to reveal to us.

Instead of spending your life on the surface of the Word, God's desire for you is to be caught in the undercurrent as it pulls you deeper and deeper into the knowledge, understanding, and revelation of His truth. Someone once asked, "When it comes to gathering golden nuggets from God's Word, are you a raker or a digger?" Simply put, do you just *read* the Bible? Or do you *study* the Bible? This question is asked, not in an attempt to put all the Bible "rakers" on a guilt trip, pointing out how much more spiritual the "diggers" are. The truth is, we all need to do both.

Bible reading is refreshing to the soul and spirit. Reading the Scriptures is like drinking a refreshing, cold glass of water on a hot day to satisfy your thirst. Thus, reading the Bible satisfies the thirst of the soul. On the other hand, Bible study is for depth. Those who study demonstrate a hunger and thirst for knowledge, a hunger for truth. Jesus said, "Man shall not live by bread alone, but by every word that proceedeth out of the mouth of God" (Matthew 4:4). Knowing your Bible, both deep and wide, brings a richness unmatched. Bible reading and Bible studying are twin disciplines; they complement each other. To understand the Bible, we need to pick it up and read it. That may sound obvious, but so many Christians simply do not do it. They go days without reading the holy Scriptures that have been given to them by God to bring them to a state of completeness in Him.

Studying the Bible gives us the opportunity to dig deeper into the Scriptures and be a witness to the greatness of God and all He has accomplished for us. Through studying, reflection, meditation, and revelation provided by the Holy Spirit, we can begin to understand the importance of each event that is written in each of the books of the Bible and how they all connect. Moreover, as we study the Scriptures and dig even deeper, we begin to understand who we are as Christians, and the life that God, through Jesus, has provided for us. When I was younger in the Lord, and occasionally still today, I would commit to an exercise to test my comprehension. How much was I retaining within my spirit and soul? I would study for as long as the Lord led me to study. Afterward, I would walk away for about an hour. Then I would return to my study with a notepad and pen and begin to take notes, writing down what the Holy Spirit was bringing back to my remembrance. After all of my notes were completed, I would go back to the

Scriptures and compare my notes to what I had studied, to see just how much I had retained. I was astonished at how much I had retained with the Holy Spirit's help.

Over time, I noticed that what the Holy Spirit revealed to me, I didn't forget, and I was able to apply His teachings to my life. Throughout the years, I have often shared with people how I learned more from the Scriptures in my personal devotion and study time at home with the Holy Spirit than I ever learned in a weekly church setting listening to a pastor. I encourage the congregants I pastor today to make time for the Lord daily. God wants you to make the daily sacrifice to seek Him. Jesus did not say that "man" will teach you all things and bring all things to your remembrance; He said the "Holy Spirit" would "teach you all things and bring all things to your remembrance" (John14:26).

Reading the Word is a necessary first step for Christians. If reading God's Word is not a regular practice in your life, then the more difficult process of studying will be nearly impossible. Reading the Bible gives us the chance to intimately connect with God and take in His glory and goodness. So often we pastors and teachers encourage our parishioners to simply read the Bible. In the past, I, too, have been guilty of that, instead of instructing them

## Growth through Knowledge

to set time aside daily for the Holy Spirit, to study and learn from Him. Jesus said, "Take my yoke upon you, and learn of me" (Matthew 11:29). Are you seeking Him? Are you meditating on what you have studied or read? Are you memorizing Scripture? To become what God has saved you to be, you must cultivate a relationship with the Holy Spirit as He instructs us and gives us a true interpretation of the holy Scriptures.

# PART IV

*Maintaining Your Relationship with God*

# PART IV

# CHAPTER 12

## *Living by Faith*

It is written: "For we walk by faith, not by sight" (2 Corinthians 5:7). The faith walk is a life not determined by what a person visualizes with the eyes, but it is a life lived on the foundation of God's Word and His promises. It is a life that is lived through Jesus in the power of the Holy Spirit as we trust God the Father to meet every need in our spiritual and physical lives. Faith is fundamental to all our experiences with God. From the moment of our physical birth, we have attempted to live our lives trusting in human nature, and we have failed. Human logic and reasoning, which is influenced by the flesh and by sin, is in constant rebellion, or at war, against God. However, after being born again, our confidence and faith is no longer in human nature, but rather, in Jesus Christ. We depend on Him to be our life, source, strength, and supplier. We must rely on God and His Word constantly as we continue on the journey of life.

*Faith* is defined as "a firm persuasion," or a "conviction based upon hearing." It is having complete trust or confidence in God. Are we totally convinced and persuaded that all the promises of God are yes and amen? I always enjoy referring to Abraham's life experience, which gives us an illustration of faith. See what was written by Paul in the book of Romans about Abraham:

> And being not weak in faith, he considered not his own body now dead, when he was about an hundred years old, neither yet the deadness of Sarah's womb: He staggered not at the promise of God through unbelief but was strong in faith, giving glory to God; and being fully persuaded that, what he had promised, he was able to perform.
>
> **—Romans 4:19–21**

In the above passage of Scripture, Paul give a brief synopsis of an encounter Abraham experienced with the Lord God. The actual account of this event can be found in Genesis 17:15 through 18:15. God had promised Abraham that his wife, Sarah, would conceive a son. At the time, Abraham was one hundred years old, and Sarah was ninety. Looking at their natural bodies, both were well past the years of childbearing. At first mention of this promise, Abraham fell upon his face in laughter, probably pondering the thought of how this could be, considering their ages. Later, in Genesis 18, Sarah, upon hearing this announcement from God, also was filled with laughter (verse

12), but our God is the God of the impossible! As Paul stated, Abraham was not weak in faith, and he did not consider his age or the status of Sarah's womb. Let's pause for a moment and speak on *not being weak in faith*. From the first day God called Abraham, he trusted in God's Word and responded accordingly. From departing his country and going to an unknown land to which God led him, or offering his son Isaac as a sacrifice to God on Mount Moriah, Abraham was obedient to everything God asked him to do. Every time God revealed Himself and showed Himself strong in Abraham life, his faith grew stronger. Remember, we live by faith; some things that God leads us to do may not make sense to us logically. However, God knows our journey and the plans He has for our lives. We must trust His Word by faith.

Abraham "staggered not" at the promises of God through doubt and unbelief, but he was strong in his faith. Understand that worry, doubt, fear, and unbelief will prevent you from receiving God's promises in your life. They are a hindrance to the fulfillment of God's promises. Those virtues come from within the flesh, from the sin nature, and from the evil one—the devil. But Abraham was fully persuaded, totally convinced, that God would do exactly what He said He would do. Likewise, we must be fully persuaded, knowing that whatever God has promised He is able to do, no matter what the circumstances are or may be. We must stand strong in faith.

Paul described his converted life in Christ this way: "I am crucified with Christ: nevertheless I live; yet not I, but Christ liveth in me: and the life which I now live in the flesh I live by the faith of the Son of God, who loved me, and gave himself for me" (Galatians 2:20). In the context of this passage, Paul explains that his old mannerisms and way of living have been put to death, crucified with Christ, and a new life in Christ has begun. This new life is not governed by fleshly properties, but rather, it is in Christ. Christ is living my life for me and through me. Therefore, my new life is now lived by faith in the Son of God.

The Scriptures tell us that "faith cometh by hearing, and hearing by the word of God" (Romans 10:17). Over time, as a person studies and hears the Word, the Holy Spirit will engraft it within the soul, and that person's faith will grow. This explains the various degrees or levels of faith operating within different individuals. The Scriptures speak of little faith, great faith, seed faith, strong faith, and a full assurance of faith. Your faith should grow. Paul wrote these words to the Church: "We are bound to thank God always for you, brethren, as it is meet, because that your faith groweth exceedingly" (2 Thessalonians 1:3). Therefore, faith is a living principle that must be constantly fed by the Word and fertilized by testing (see James 1:3 and 1 Peter 1:7).

To continue to define the word *faith*, it is a voluntary response to God's Word whereby every Christian places the weight of his need upon a trusted object—that object being Christ Jesus. Jesus Christ must be the object of our faith—He whom the writer of Hebrews stated is "the author and finisher of our faith" (Hebrews 12:2). Simply put, faith is placing your trust, confidence, and life in Christ's hands. Keep in mind the seed principle. For a seed to germinate and produce life and grow, it must first be watered. Likewise, we know that faith is a living principle, and for it to properly grow, it must be watered daily with the reading and studying of the Word.

Faith is so important to the believer that God reveals on numerous occasions that the "just shall live by faith." The first time we see this phrase is in the book of Habakkuk: "the just shall live by his faith" (Habakkuk 2:4). However, this is also stated in Romans 1:17, Hebrews 10:38, and 2 Corinthians 5:7. We know there is no forgiveness of sins without the shed blood of Jesus. But faith is just as important to the Christian because there will be no relationship and no way of pleasing God without faith. The Scriptures go as far to tell us that "without faith it is impossible to [walk with God and] please Him, for whoever comes [near] to God must [necessarily] believe that God exists and that He rewards those who [earnestly and diligently] seek Him" (Hebrews 11:6 AMP). There are many things we petition God for in prayer but our request is not answered. Many would respond to this by saying it "was not meant to be," but they never question their faith level, whether that is hindering them from receiving from God what they are asking Him for.

In the book of Matthew, we read about two blind men who sought Jesus for healing. The Bible states:

> And when Jesus departed thence, two blind men followed him, crying, and saying, Thou son of David, have mercy on us. And when he was come into the house, the blind men came to him: and Jesus saith unto them, Believe ye that I am able to do this? They said unto him, Yea, Lord. Then touched he their eyes, saying, According to your faith be it unto you. And their eyes were opened.
>
> **—Matthew 9:27–30**

Over the years, the church community has gleaned the phrase "blind faith" from this story, as these two men followed Jesus into a house even though physically they could not see Him. Upon their arrival at the house, Jesus asked them, "Believe that I am able to do this?" Every time we seek God for something—especially something that's impossible for man to do—God asks you, very simply, as He asked them, "Do you believe I am able to do this?" Your answer may determine whether your prayer request will be answered.

Without hesitation, the men in Jesus' day answered, "Yes, Lord," and Jesus replied, "According to your faith be it unto you." When confronted with the same question, you may also answer, "Yes, Lord," but then immediately the onus is shifted to your faith. Is your faith at the level to receive from God that for which you are praying? In reading this encounter of the blind men and Jesus, I speculate what might have happened if they didn't have the level of faith needed to receive the healing of their sight. Would Jesus have healed them anyway? Something to consider.

## Faith and Works

Regarding this topic, I want to briefly address faith and works. Is just having faith enough? Often in Scripture, *faith* is accompanied by *works*. "Works" refers to a corresponding action to that which has been revealed to you by faith. Simply put, you respond to what has been revealed to you by faith—you act on it. Along this spiritual journey, you may have overheard people say they are "believing God" for something; however, they are not doing anything to position themselves to receive that for which they are asking or believing. The apostle James shares with us the need for faith and works:

> What doth it profit, my brethren, though a man say he hath faith, and have not works? can faith save him? If a brother or sister be naked, and destitute of daily food, and one of you say unto them, Depart in peace, be ye warmed and filled; notwithstanding ye give them not those things which are needful to the body; what doth it profit? Even so faith, if it hath not works, is dead, being alone. Yea, a man may say, Thou hast faith, and I have works: shew me thy faith without thy works, and I will shew thee my faith by my works.
>
> —**James 2:14–18**

If a person proclaims they have faith, their faith should be proven by what they do. Sadly, far too often we have seen and heard of people—even those who truly have a need—be turned away by those in the church. We are so quick to say, "I'll be praying for you," rather providing the individual with what's needed to sustain them at that moment. I have known Christians who had the resources to assist someone, but they were unwilling to part with their own money, clothes, or food. A selfish person will never be blessed! We have forgotten the words of Jesus when He said, "It is more blessed to give than to receive" (Acts 20:35).

God always challenges us to come out of our comfort zones, to make a sacrifice and do something we normally wouldn't do. We can talk as if we have faith, but as the Scriptures have said, "Show me your faith without your works, and I will show you my faith by my works"—in other words, by what I do. In fact, Scripture proves that your faith *can* be seen by what you do.

In the gospel of Mark, Jesus was in the city of Capernaum conducting a service within a house (Mark 2:1–12). The house was full to capacity, and no one else could fit in, but Jesus preached the Word to all who were there. Remember, faith comes by hearing, and hearing by the Word of God.

While Jesus was preaching, four men carrying a man sick with the palsy attempted to get in, but they could not because the house was full. Unlike many today who have given up, believing it just wasn't meant to be, these men were persistent and determined to see Jesus—so much so that the man with the palsy convinced those carrying him to uncover the roof, breaking up the structure, then rig up a system to lower the man down into the presence of Jesus. At that, the Bible said, "Jesus saw their faith" (Mark 2:5). Well, you may ask, how did Jesus see their faith? Jesus saw their faith by what they did to get the man into His presence—in other words, their works. Due to this act of faith accompanied by works, not only was the man healed, but his sins were also forgiven (Mark 2:5–11).

If you are believing God to open a door for you to obtain a job, after praying about it, get up and turn in some job applications! If it's healing you need, get up and do what you can—don't just lie around in bed complaining. No, in the name of Jesus, speak healing into your life and minister to someone else who is seeking healing as well. Your words, spoken with faith, have power. Remember, faith without works is dead!

## The Power of Your Words

Just as the sword of the Spirit is activated by speaking the Word aloud, so is your faith. Thus, we must be mindful of the words we speak when we are in the midst of life's challenges. After Jesus had made His triumphal entry into

## Living by Faith

Jerusalem, which began the week of His passion, concluding at the cross, one of the final lessons He would teach His disciples was concerning the power of their words. The narrative is found in the gospel of Mark:

> And on the morrow, when they were come from Bethany, he was hungry: And seeing a fig tree afar off having leaves, he came, if haply he might find any thing thereon: and when he came to it, he found nothing but leaves; for the time of figs was not yet. And Jesus answered and said unto it, No man eat fruit of thee hereafter for ever, And his disciples heard it.
>
> **—Mark 11:12–14**

The story centers around a barren fig tree. Jesus cursed this tree because it was not bearing any fruit. What's intriguing to me is the fact that not only did Jesus actually have a conversation with this fig tree, but the tree evidently had words for Jesus! The text states that Jesus "answered and said unto it . . ." You cannot "answer" someone without them having spoken to you first. Obviously, Jesus was not happy with the response the tree was giving Him regarding not bearing fruit, and therefore He cursed it. His disciples were with Him, and they heard Him curse the fig tree by saying, "No man shall eat fruit from you forever."

## Now That I Have Been Born Again, *What's Next?*

Jesus intentionally did this in the presence of His disciples to use it as a teaching moment. The narrative continues:

> And in the morning, as they passed by, they saw the fig tree dried up from the roots. And Peter calling to remembrance saith unto him, Master, behold, the fig tree which thou cursed is withered away. And Jesus answering saith unto them, Have faith in God. For verily I say unto you, That whosoever shall say unto this mountain, Be thou removed, and be thou cast into the sea; and shall not doubt in his heart, but shall believe that those things which he saith shall come to pass, he shall have whatsoever he saith. Therefore I say unto you, What things soever ye desire, when ye pray, believe that ye receive them, and ye shall have them.
>
> **—Mark 11:20–24**

Although the disciples didn't say anything to Jesus, they likely spoke among themselves about what they had just witnessed, and the next day, they were looking forward to passing by the fig tree, just to see if Jesus' words would come to fruition. With eagerness, they passed by the fig tree, and they noticed with amazement that it had withered from the roots! Peter immediately said to Jesus, "The fig tree which You cursed is completely dried up and withered away!" Jesus responded by saying, "Have faith in God." This phrase could also be translated, "Have the faith of God" or "the God kind of faith." Jesus always sought out ways to teach and give instruction to His disciples—just as He is currently seeking to teach and give the Church instruction today. Jesus is the example for us to follow.

After encouraging them to have faith in God, in the next verse, three times He placed emphasis on the words "say" and "saith": "Whosoever shall say to this mountain . . ." (Mark 11:23). Jesus was referring to the obstacles, problems, challenges, and difficulties we experience in life. In the power and authority of the name of Jesus, we are told to speak to our problems, hindrances, sicknesses, and challenges, sending them away and not doubting or operating in the spirit of unbelief as we do so. In this way, we can have "whatsoever we say," according to the will of God for our lives.

Jesus continued by saying, "What things soever ye desire, when ye pray, believe that ye receive them, and ye shall have them" (Mark 11:24). The moment we begin to petition God in the name of Jesus for something, we should believe that that something is manifested even though we have not yet physically or tangibly received it. I have always said that if you cannot see yourself obtaining the victory or deliverance in the spiritual realm, you will not procure it in the physical realm. It all begins with speaking words of faith over your life and the challenges you are facing, *knowing* God can deliver you.

Even so, although it may seem as if you are doing everything right, persecution for Christ will still occur, so remain steadfast and keep the faith! In the next chapter, we will look at this persecution we will face as we maintain our faith.

# CHAPTER 13

## *A Life of Persecution*

Yea, and all that will live godly in Christ Jesus shall suffer persecution.

—**2 Timothy 3:12**

My mother would always tell me that with every rose, there are thorns. Being in a loving relationship with the Father through Jesus is the greatest experience a person will ever have. However, because of your relationship with Christ, persecution and suffering *will* follow. You are a child of light, which makes you a minority living in the realm of darkness—where the devil is the prince—and so the battle has begun. Over the years, many new Christians, as well as some who have been in faith for years, have come to me, saying, "Pastor, it seems as if I am constantly being persecuted . . . constantly under attack." One gentleman went so far as to say that his problems immediately began after he received and accepted the revelation of truth from the Scriptures. Understand this: suffering persecution for the sake of Christ is a badge of honor, so don't become frustrated or discouraged when it occurs. I always say, if you aren't doing what is right, then the devil would not be messing with you!

*Persecution* means "to harass, trouble, mistreat, and to pursue and seek after eagerly." For Christians, persecution may come from friends, family members, from any others who are not pleased with your decision to become a follower of Christ, and from those who are not saved. Keep in mind that the enemy of your soul is not happy with you walking away from him and accepting Jesus as the Lord of your life.

In the above passage of Scripture, Paul was writing to Timothy to encourage him. He told his young friend, "If you live a godly life, you will suffer persecution." In searching the Scriptures, we see that all of God's people have been persecuted at some time or another. Even our Savior, Jesus Himself, was persecuted, as well as were His apostles. In fact, Jesus said in the Sermon on the Mount, "Blessed are ye, when men shall revile you, and persecute you, and shall say all manner of evil against you falsely, for my sake. Rejoice, and be exceeding glad: for great is your reward in heaven: for so persecuted they the prophets which were before you" (Matthew 5:11–12). If you have been saved, and if there is an anointing upon your life, then the devil is going to do everything in his power to abort what God has placed within you.

## A Life of Persecution

Persecution can come in various ways—through lies, through deception, through mistreatment by those who say they love you, from harassment by those on your job, and from predators who tempt you to commit sinful acts. The moment you surrendered your life to Christ, you entered conflict—a war for your very soul. The devil wants you back, and the only way he can come between you and God is to cause you to sin. Thus, a life of obedience to God's Word and His will is paramount. As I stated earlier in this writing, sin separates us from God. As believers, we cannot not allow persecution and suffering to overwhelm us. The Scripture says, "Beloved, think it not strange concerning the fiery trial which is to try you, as though some strange thing happened unto you: But rejoice, inasmuch as ye are partakers of Christ's sufferings" (1 Peter 4:12–13). Many Christians complain about what they are going through when they should be rejoicing in the Lord and thanking Him for the victory!

During times of persecution and suffering, the Bible encourages us to "submit yourselves therefore to God. Resist the devil, and he will flee from you" (James 4:7). We submit ourselves to God through prayer, fasting, rejoicing, praising, worshiping, and giving Him thanks. The tempter and oppressor will flee, but we must continue to be in a state of submission to God because our enemy, the devil, will certainly return. Remember, only the Lord can keep you and deliver you, as the Scriptures declare, "The Lord is faithful, who shall stablish you, and keep you from evil" (2 Thessalonians 3:3).

Gaining an understanding of why Christians suffer begins with considering the suffering of our Lord and the salvation we secured through Him, which produced a new life within us. In the book of 1 Peter, the apostle, under the guidance of the Holy Spirit, informs us about suffering and persecution:

> Forasmuch then as Christ hath suffered for us in the flesh, arm yourselves likewise with the same mind: for he that hath suffered in the flesh hath ceased from sin; that he no longer should live the rest of his time in the flesh to the lusts of men, but to the will of God. For the time past of our life may suffice us to have wrought the will of the Gentiles, when we walked in lasciviousness, lusts, excess of wine, revellings, banquetings, and abominable idolatries: Wherein they think it strange that ye run not with them to the same excess of riot, speaking evil of you.
>
> —1 Peter 4:1–4

## A Life of Persecution

There is so much to unpack here. These four verses speak of suffering in the flesh and enduring persecution because of Christ and our willingness to follow Him. The inner struggles and persecution we face from within, as well as the external persecution from those whom the enemy sends on assignment to disrupt our lives, can be daunting. So, let's begin with the fact that Christ suffered for us in the flesh, and we should have the same mindset when it comes to suffering. The Lord Jesus is the pattern and example every Christian must follow, even in times of suffering and persecution. In His own suffering, Christ demonstrated patience, submissiveness, and obedience despite the unjust treatment from those He created. Men lied about Him, spat upon Him, beat Him with a whip, and hung our Lord on a cross. This was undeserved, unjust treatment that Jesus received. However, He was patient and submissive to God the Father, understanding His purpose and what He was sent to do. Jesus never complained during His time of persecution and suffering. In Hebrews, it is written, "Lo, I come (in the volume of the book it is written of me), to do thy will, O God" (Hebrews 10:7). And how can we forget what the Scriptures say concerning Jesus: "Though he were a Son, yet learned he obedience by the things which he suffered" (Hebrews 5:8). Obedience is a learned behavior, and we cannot learn obedience without suffering.

## Now That I Have Been Born Again, *What's Next?*

The apostle Peter's attitude toward unjust suffering is found in these words: "For it is better, if the will of God be so, that ye suffer for well doing, than for evil doing" (1 Peter 3:17). Christians are implored to demonstrate this same mindset when we face persecution and suffering. We are to arm ourselves simply, meaning we are to be completely dressed in the spiritual armor, and we are to have the same attitude and mindset toward unjust suffering as Jesus did. The Christian who has suffered in the flesh is the Christian who has suffered ill treatment or unjust treatment from those who are in darkness, from those who are of the world, from sinners. This unjust treatment is the result of the saintly desire to forsake sin and live a holy life in Christ Jesus through the power of the Holy Spirit. Attacks from the enemy of our souls will come, and the only way we will endure and overcome them is by having the attitude Jesus had when it came to suffering and persecution.

When we have the same attitude toward suffering and persecution as Jesus, our desire is to live the reminder of our earthly lives according to the will of God and not to the flesh and the lust of men. The moment we were saved, God broke the power of the sinful nature that once ruled our lives. Jesus, our Sin Bearer, bore our sins in His body, totally obliterating the sinful nature and rendering it powerless. The saint who is saved is immersed in—meaning

## A Life of Persecution

baptized into—Christ by the Holy Spirit, thus partaking of all Jesus accomplished for us through His death and resurrection. Having the sinful nature now rendered powerless, the Christian seeks to live the duration of his life to the will of God.

Now that you are no longer living to fulfill the lust of the flesh—including getting high, worshiping material possessions, and living in the spirit of wantonness without restraint—your old friends will now speak evil of you. They ridicule you because you are not willing to participate in these activities with them as you once did. In time, the Lord will align you with new friends who love Him as you do, and you will provide strength to one another in your journey in Christ. As the proverb states, "Iron sharpeneth iron; so a man sharpeneth the countenance of his friend" (Proverbs 27:17). I know it can be a daily challenge, because we all want to feel accepted by our friends and peers. However, nowhere in Scripture does it say that living the Christian life will be easy—because it's not. Jesus said, "If any man will come after me, let him deny himself, and take up his cross, and follow me" (Matthew 16:24).

As we finish this chapter on persecution and suffering—which is something you will experience for the remainder of your earthly life—remember that you are not alone in this battle. The Holy Spirit is forever present with you. Honestly, it is not your fight—it is the Lord's battle, and He will fight for you if you submit to Him. As the apostle Peter wrote, "Yet if any man suffer as a Christian, let him not be ashamed; but let him glorify God on this behalf" (1 Peter 4:16). No matter what people may say, what they might assume, or how they may question why you are experiencing suffering, hold your head up and do not be ashamed. The only One to whom you must give an account is God. Every Christian is traveling the same road, although our trials, suffering, and persecutions vary due to our different callings, purposes, and anointings. Continue to stand in your faith and on God's promises, trusting Him, and remember these three passages of scripture:

> Ye are of God, little children, and have overcome them: because greater is he that is in you, than he that is in the world.
>
> —**1 John 4:4**

> What shall we then say to these things? If God be for us, who can be against us?
>
> —**Romans 8:31**

> Nay, in all these things we are more than conquerors through him that loved us.
>
> —**Romans 8:37**

## A Life of Persecution

Amid persecution and suffering, remain steadfast and stand firm on the Word of God. Continue to press forward toward the mark of the prize of the high calling of God in Christ Jesus: "But he that shall endure unto the end, the same shall be saved" (Matthew 24:13).

# CHAPTER 14

## *Working Out Your Salvation*

> Wherefore, my beloved, as ye have always obeyed, not as in my presence only, but now much more in my absence, work out your own salvation with fear and trembling.
>
> **—Philippians 2:12**

Previously, I stated that salvation happens the moment we confess and repent of our sins, and accept Jesus as Lord of our lives. The apostle Paul wrote, "That if thou shalt confess with thy mouth the Lord Jesus, and shalt believe in thine heart that God hath raised him from the dead, thou shalt be saved. For with the heart man believeth unto righteousness; and with the mouth confession is made unto salvation. . . . For whosoever shall call upon the name of the Lord shall be saved" (Romans 10:9–10, 13). When we translate the word "saved" here from the Greek, we get the word *sozo*. Likewise, the Greek translation of the word "salvation" is *soteria*. Looking at the definition of both of these Greek words from *Vine's Expository Dictionary of Biblical Words*, we see they each imply deliverance. Spiritual and eternal deliverance is immediately granted by

God to those who accept His conditions of repentance and faith in the Lord Jesus, in whom alone salvation is to be obtained.

I have also mentioned that sanctification is a lifelong process. *Sanctification* meaning "separation unto God" is used in the New Testament to represent the separation of the believer from evil things and behavior. We were saved to become Christlike and to live a Christlike life while we are here on the earth as we submit to the Lordship of Christ. We are depending on the Holy Spirit to aid us in this transformation process because it could not happen without Him; however, we must also do our part.

In Philippians 2:12, Paul wrote to the saints at Philippi, encouraging them to live a life of obedience and to continue to conduct themselves as citizens of heaven should. Jesus told His disciples to pray, "Thy kingdom come, Thy will be done in earth, as it is in heaven" (Matthew 6:10). Let's address the words "Thy kingdom come." This kingdom, the Kingdom of God, officially came to the earth after the death, burial, and resurrection of Jesus. It is a spiritual Kingdom of Light, in which every believer is placed the moment they are saved. Our Lord said, "Behold, the kingdom of God is within you" (Luke 17:21). God reigns within the souls and spirits of believers through the indwelling Holy Spirit and the engrafted Word. Therefore, since the Kingdom of God is within us, His will should also be done in us, just as it is in heaven. We are Kingdom citizens governed by Kingdom principles to which we must adhere. We have been delivered from the power of darkness and have been translated into the Kingdom of his dear Son (Colossians 1:13).

In Philippians 2:12, Paul commended them for their constant obedience. What validates our love for God is our obedience to Him. Jesus said, "If you love me, keep my commandments" (John 14:15). Walking in truth can be challenging, especially when it convicts you of something you are not quite ready to release or if it conflicts with your lifestyle. God uses His Word in the process of cleaning us and setting us apart from the world so that we can be used of Him. However, we must be willing to receive the truth and conform to it. Jesus said, "Now ye are clean through the word which I have spoken unto you" (John 15:3), and "sanctify them through thy truth: thy word is truth" (John 17:17). Keep in mind there will be no disobedient or rebellious people present in God's Kingdom.

Paul continues his discourse to the saints by telling them to "work out your own salvation." As I unpack all that's contained in these five words—and there is a lot—

let's begin with what these five words do *not* mean. They do *not* mean that we are to work for our salvation, for two reasons. First, the people whom Paul was ministering to were already saved. Second, man has no ability, nor power to save himself from the bondage, guilt, and penalty of sin. Salvation is a work of God for mankind, a work that has already been accomplished and fulfilled by Jesus at the cross. Man cannot merit salvation through his self-righteous deeds, which Isaiah described as "filthy rags" (Isaiah 64:6).

When we look at the words "work out" here, we see they are the translation of a Greek word that means "to carry out to the goal," or "to carry to its ultimate conclusion." The saints at Philippi, just as we are today, were exhorted to carry their salvation to its ultimate conclusion, or goal, which is Christlikeness. Paul was not referring to salvation in the form of justification, but he was referring to sanctification, to victory over sin, and to living a life that's pleasing to the Lord Jesus. Again, sanctification is a lifelong process, and we must remember that only God, through the Holy Spirit, who gives the revelation of truth, can bring us to the point of Christlikeness as we submit to Him and walk in obedience to His Word.

Next, Paul placed an emphasis on the words "own salvation." Your walk and relationship with God are personal. If you have been saved, then Jesus is your Lord and your personal Savior. Everyone has been granted one life in which they must find their way back home to God the Father. We have only one lifetime to get it right.

Those who play recreational golf are familiar with the word *mulligan*. A *mulligan* is an extra stroke allowed after a poor shot, and it is not counted on the score card. Well, despite the rules of golf, in life you are not allowed a mulligan; no one is allowed a second chance after their physical death. Oftentimes, people become consumed with critiquing someone else's life instead of working on their own. You have only one lifetime to work on *you*, so make sure *you* are in alignment with God. God will not tolerate nor justify sin in the life of a believer in Christ. We must live a holy, sanctified life through Christ.

We read Scriptures that say things like, "As it is written, There is none righteous, no, not one" (Romans 3:10), and "For all have sinned, and come short of the glory of God" (Romans 3:23), and "If we say that we have no sin, we deceive ourselves, and the truth is not in us" (1 John 1:8). Often, many believers use these passages of Scripture to justify the sin in their lives, not realizing that these verses *actually* speak of your life prior to your conversion, prior

## Now That I Have Been Born Again, *What's Next?*

to you becoming saved. God's preference is that you, the believer, no longer practice sin in your life.

Let's allow the Scriptures to speak for themselves:

> My little children, these things write I unto you, that ye sin not.
>
> **—1 John 2:1**

> Whosoever abideth in him sinneth not: whosoever sinneth hath not seen him, neither known him.
>
> **—1 John 3:6**

> Whosoever is born of God doth not commit sin; for his seed remaineth in him: and he cannot sin, because he is born of God.
>
> **—1 John 3:9**

> We know that whosoever is born of God sinneth not; but he that is begotten of God keepeth himself, and that wicked one toucheth him not.
>
> **—1 John 5:18**

> Awake to righteousness, and sin not; for some have the knowledge of God: I speak this to your shame
>
> **—1 Corinthians 15:34**

## Working Out Your Salvation

After reading these passages of Scripture, you may feel as if a life of holiness is impossible, but would God demand something that's impossible to achieve? The woman who was caught in the very act of adultery, after Jesus forgave her sin, He told her to "go, and sin no more" (John 8:11). Likewise, the man who lay at the pool of Bethesda, waiting for the troubling of the water, was told, after Jesus healed him, "Sin no more, lest a worse thing come unto thee" (John 5:14). Again, did Jesus tell them to do something that was impossible? Nowhere in Scripture will you find it written that God is okay with you constantly missing the mark, falling short, or sinning.

Understand, God does not want believers to practice sinning or to habitually commit acts of sin. I am a firm believer that acts of sin by believers is the main reason there is a "power shortage" within the Church today. We don't experience a plethora of spiritual healings, miracles, signs and wonders, and spiritual gifts among the church community because we have become unplugged from the Source of power—the Holy Spirit. Sin restricts the flow of the Holy Spirit's power. With that being said, let's return to 1 John: "These things write I unto you, that ye sin not. And if any man sin, we have an advocate with the Father, Jesus Christ the righteous" (1 John 2:1). I want to address the phrase "if any man sin." First, it does not say, "if any man commits sins"; it states "if any man sin." *Sin* here is singular, referring to one single act or event. When a believer sins, he or she should immediately confess and repent of that sin, and our Advocate (a legal term, referring to a lawyer or one who represents you), Jesus, will petition our case to God the Father.

The writer of Hebrews declared: "Let us lay aside every weight, and the sin which doth so easily beset us" (Hebrews 12:1). The saint should lay aside every hindrance and sin—and again, *sin* is singular, not *sins*. *Repentance* means "to turn from something and to turn to something else." Simply put, a person who repents of a sin has a change of heart; they turn from that sin and then turn to God. Their true repentance must involve forsaking that sin. For example, if a Christian has committed fornication, but he goes to God and truly repents of that sin, he should then completely forsake it and never commit that sin again. We in the fivefold ministry have done believers a disservice when it comes to equipping them for the life ahead by not telling them the truth. At the end of the day, it's not going to be about the sermons you have preached or heard, the songs you have sung, even the money you have given or how many times you've attended church—it's going to be about the life you lived daily before God and man. Jesus shares with us some interesting words in Matthew's gospel:

> Not every one that saith unto me, Lord, Lord, shall enter into the kingdom of heaven, but he that doeth the will of my Father which is in heaven. Many will say to me in that day, Lord, Lord, have we not prophesied in thy name? And in thy name have cast out devils? And in thy name done many wonderful works? And then will I profess unto them, I never knew you: depart from me, ye that work iniquity.
>
> **—Matthew 7:21–23**

The answer to these questions Jesus has asked is found in Matthew 25:34–40; take a moment to read these verses. People are often so busy trying to make a name for themselves, or, as they say today, "growing their brand," that they have forgotten that the main reason for divine empowerment from the Holy Spirit was in order to live a Christlike life.

Christians must allow the Holy Spirit to daily govern their lives and affairs. Paul instructed the saints to "walk in the Spirit, and ye shall not fulfill the lust of the flesh" (Galatians 5:16), and that was followed with this directive: "If we live in the Spirit, let us also walk in the Spirit" (Galatians 5:25). We must remember that just as God the Father and God the Son are holy, likewise is God the Holy Spirit.

He cannot be tempted with evil, and neither will he tempt people with evil (James 1:12–14).

The word *walk* found in Galatians 5:25 is a military term meaning "to be in step with." You must be in step with the Holy Spirit. You have received your marching orders; they are: do not commit sin, and live a life of holiness. Now you are standing at attention and waiting for the command to march. When the command is given by the Holy Spirit to march, move ahead with urgency and remain obedient! Do not deviate to the right or to the left; stay in step, and in doing so, you will not fall or fulfill the desires of the flesh.

We sin when we step out the will of God and try to do things our way. When we say no to the devil or to our flesh, we must truly mean it. We must trust the Holy Spirit to navigate us through the season of testing. Again, for the believer in Christ, sin is no longer a *lifestyle*, because we are not governed by the sin nature. However, God never took away our freedom of choice, and in the midst of testing, suffering, and persecution, we must choose to do what's right. Transformation and sanctification do not take place overnight; they involve a lifelong process, so continue to seek the Lord.

Paul wrote, "If ye then be risen with Christ, seek those things which are above, where Christ sitteth on the right hand of God. Set your affection on things above, not on things on the earth. For ye are dead, and your life is hid with Christ in God. When Christ, who is our life, shall appear, then shall ye also appear with him in glory" (Colossians 3:1-4). We are seated in heavenly places in Christ; therefore, we can live a life of freedom simply because we are in Him. Our love should be for things above and no longer for earthly, worldly things. Continue in His love and remain faithful amid life's challenges.

During your life in Christ, you will experience growth spurts. At times, you may feel as if you are moving forward; other times, you may feel as if you are barely creeping along. Either way, *continue to press forward!* The Lord will be with you throughout the entire process. Jesus said, "I will never leave thee, nor forsake thee" (Hebrews 13:5).

\*\*\*

I pray the words I have shared in this book will help you as you travel the narrow road. Keep the faith and having done all to stand, stand. I would like to close this work with a passage of Scripture found in 2 Corinthians: "Therefore, whether we are at home [on earth] or away from home [and with Him], it is our [constant] ambition to be pleasing to Him" (2 Corinthians 5:9 AMP). God bless you on your journey of life in Christ!

# ABOUT THE AUTHOR

**Pastor Kenneth Polk**, a teacher of God's Word, was saved in the summer of 1979. Pastor Ken accepted Christ as his personal Savior at Anderson Memorial Church of God in Christ, under the pastorate of the late bishop C.L. Anderson. The realization that God had a special mission for him to fulfill became apparent the very Sunday he was saved. As he was walking out of the church, he placed his hand on the door to push it open, he heard the voice of the Lord saying, *This is a new beginning—go out and face the world!* From that moment, his life was transformed. It is truly by the grace of God that he has become the man he is today.

Pastor Ken received his ministerial calling in 1981 while attending Christ Covenant Church, where the late Arthur L. Gooden was the pastor. In 1982, Pastor Ken enrolled in Detroit Bible College. In the late 1980s, the college changed its name to William Tyndale College. He left Bible college after two years and completed his ministerial training under the tutelage of Pastor Gooden. Through much study of and revelations from Scripture, originating from the Holy Spirit, he was ordained into the ministry of the Gospel in 1984. He became the assistant pastor at

Christ Covenant Church in 1987 and served in that capacity until November 1999. In December 1999, Pastor Ken became the pastor of Followers of Christ Christian Center.

Followers of Christ is a teaching ministry. Using the Bible as his textbook, Pastor Ken is committed to training and preparing God's people to live a holy, righteous life. This is accomplished by teaching truth and not compromising the Word of God. On March 13, 2020, due to the stay-at-home mandates caused by the COVID-19 pandemic, the doors of the church were shut. Because this was a small ministry, it has yet to reopen, but Pastor Ken continues to proclaim the Gospel message nonetheless, especially via the internet, as his teaching is heard daily on the streaming service Live 365. The program is titled *Followers of Christ*.

For the past three years, Pastor Ken has become more of an evangelist than a pastor, taking the message of God wherever He is sent. Pastor Ken has been blessed with the gift of teaching, which shines through in his writings. *Now That I Have Been Born Again, What's Next?* is his second book. He prays this work has encouraged and strengthened you in your walk with the Lord Jesus Christ.

Milton Keynes UK
Ingram Content Group UK Ltd.
UKHW050725180724
445674UK00015B/475